A Cheechako
Goes to the Klondike

A Cheechako
Goes to the Klondike

C. W. ADAMS

Foreword by Jack Williams   *Afterword by Jack Kutz*

ALASKA HERITAGE LIBRARY
Celebrating Northern History through Books

JOHN D. WILLIAMS TRUST / EPICENTER PRESS
Alaska Book Adventures

Publisher: Kent Sturgis
Cover and Book Design: Elizabeth Watson
Illustrators: Marilyn Jesmain, Dave Lyons
Proofreader: Sherrill Carlson
Index: Sherrill Carlson
Printer: Transcontinental printing

Library of Congress Control No. 2002110859

Cover illustrations: Marilyn Jesmain's illustrative reproduction of C.W. Adams is drawn
from a photograph and his steamer, the *Lavelle Young,* is drawn from photographs.

PRINTED IN CANADA
10 9 8 7 6 5 4 3 2 1

To order single copies of
this edition of A CHEECHAKO
GOES TO THE KLONDIKE,
mail $14.95 plus $4.95 for shipping
(WA residents add $1.30 state
sales tax) to Epicenter Press,
PO Box 82368, Kenmore, WA 98028,
or phone our 24-hour order-line at
800-950-6663. Visa, MC accepted.

Discover exciting ALASKA BOOK ADVENTURES!
Visit Epicenter's online Alaska bookstore and art gallery at www.EpicenterPress.com

Dedicated to Captain Howard L. Adams,

Elizabeth Adams Jarvi, and the family of C. W. Adams;

the Pioneers of Alaska, Igloo No. 4 and Auxiliary No. 8;

and the Fairbanks Historical Preservation Foundation.

Approximately $1.25 of the proceeds

from the sale of this book will be donated in the name

of the Charles W. Adams Family to historic restoration

and preservation in Fairbanks and Alaska.

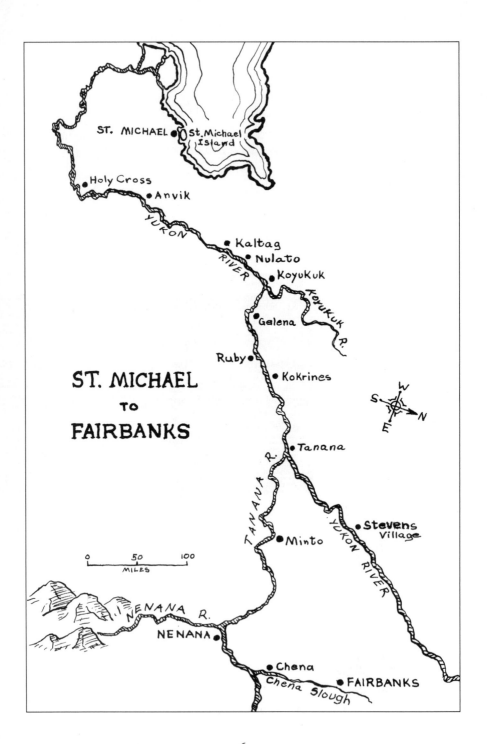

ST. MICHAEL

TO

FAIRBANKS

ST. MICHAEL
St. Michael Island
Holy Cross
Anvik
YUKON RIVER
Kaltag
Nulato
Koyukuk
KOYUKUK R.
Galena
Ruby
Kokrines
Tanana
TANANA R.
Stevens Village
Minto
YUKON RIVER
NENANA R.
NENANA
Chena
Chena Slough
FAIRBANKS

0   50   100
MILES

TABLE OF CONTENTS

GLOSSARY

BOW. Front end of boat.

STERN. The back end or "aftermost" part of the boat.

PORT. Left-hand side when looking forward.

STARBOARD. Right-hand side when looking forward.

HULL. This is the ship proper, from the main deck (either a cargo or passenger deck) at any designated distance above the waterline to the bottom of the keel. Among other things the hull contains the engines, storage space, and crew quarters.

KEEL. The backbone of the vessel and its lowest part.

TOPSIDES. The hull from the waterline to the main deck.

WATERLINE. The dividing line between the immersed part of the hull and the topsides.

HULL DEPTH. Total distance from the main deck to the bottom of the keel.

DRAFT. The distance from the waterline to the bottom of the keel. A boat may draw four feet. She will be aground if the water is only three feet deep.

DECKS. Any number of decks may be above the Main Deck. Sometimes numbered but often carrying such names as the Saloon Deck, the Passenger Deck, the Pilot House Deck, the Boiler Deck, and the Hurricane deck (the last two names commonly used on the Mississippi River).

PILOT HOUSE (Wheelhouse). This area contains the steering wheel and a signal device to give engine room orders. The signal device could be a mechanical Engine Room Telegraph with handles and bells or pull cord to "jingle" the engine room. The wheelhouse usually has a compass, a chart table, switches to control navigational lighting, whistles, searchlights, and other navigational aids.

MASTS AND BOOMS. The masts generally are vertical, fixed into the hull, and very strong. Booms, attached to the lower end of the masts, will swivel any way when held to an angle by tackle from the mast and directed by rope "gangs" from the deck.

STEAMBOAT. All machinery is operated by steam from a boiler and is very quiet.

PADDLEWHEEL. Rotating structure at stern that propels the boat, forward or backward, driven by horizontal engines alternately pushing and pulling long Pitman Arms to crank on each side of the paddlewheel.

RUDDERS. Sternwheelers generally had five rudders, three in front of the paddlewheel to "flank" stern to port or starboard when backing, and two "monkey rudders" aft of the wheel for straight ahead steering.

HOGGING. A truss shaped like an upside-down bridge was created using tall posts strung with rod or chain to stiffen the hull. These were necessary because the wooden sternwheeler hulls tended to bend and twist.

WALKING LEGS. Portable heavy logs or poles long enough to reach from the height of stifflegs (masts) port and starboard to the sand on each side of the boat. These were used with blocks and tackle to lift the bow of the boat off of sandbars.

Foreword

CHEECHAKO: North American Indian jargon word from the Chinook people of the Pacific Northwest, *t'shi*, meaning "new"; and from the Nootka people of the northwestern Canada/Vancouver Island region, *chaco*, meaning "to come"; hence, chee chaco, fr and cheechako, eng . . . *newcomer*.

⚓ ⚓ ⚓

Charles W. Adams was born in 1877, and his life span of eighty-five years encompassed perhaps the most significant global transformation in history.

In 1898, when the farm boy from North Dakota went to the Klondike as a cheechako, the quickest and least expensive way to get there was a three-part process—climb, walk, and float. Never in his wildest imaginings would Adams ever have dreamed that one day he would be able to *fly* out.

Even more incredible would have been the concept that in his mid 20s, as a key player in the founding of what would become Alaska's second-largest city, he would play a memorable role in the economic, political, and demographic transformation of the entire Territory.

⚓ ⚓ ⚓

On June 10, 1952, this cheechako from Maine arrived in Fairbanks, astounded to be in a city only twenty-nine years older than I was. It was an exciting place! It was constantly changing, seething with energy and optimism in a lifestyle of freedom and independence embraced by cheechakos and sourdoughs alike.

It was during the city's first Golden Days celebration in July that I heard of Capt. Charles Adams, the *Lavelle Young*, E.T. Barnette, Felix Pedro's gold strike, and the sequence of coincidences in my opinion too unlikely to be acceptable fiction, that led to the founding of Fairbanks. It is certain that if anyone then had predicted my future would be linked with Charles W. Adams, his history, and his family, I would have rejected it as beyond impossible. Nevertheless, that is exactly what happened.

I first learned of *A Cheechako Goes to the Klondike* in 1990 at the Alderbrook, Washington home of the author's nephew, Captain Howard Adams and his lovely wife, Lora.

Howard had succeeded his uncle Charles as master of the steamer *Nenana*, which then was being authentically restored by the Fairbanks Historical Preservation Foundation in Fairbanks. Marine consultant Jack Kutz and I were directing that five-year project and visited Howard on one of our trips for advice and information.

Howard asked if we were aware that Charles had written a book. We knew he had given an interview for an article in the *Alaska Sportsman* magazine in 1961, titled "I Hauled Fairbanks on a Sternwheeler," but we had never heard of his book. We were surprised and delighted when Howard told us the book had never been published and that he had been working for some time to get the typescript ready.

Sadly, Lora died in the spring of 1991 and Howard, after a long illness, followed in 1995. He never completed his work on *Cheechako*.

However, Capt. Howard Adams did come to Fairbanks on July 12, 1992 as guest of honor at the dedication of his beloved, restored *Nenana* and received the plaque from the National Park Service designating her as a National Historic Landmark.

This was a bittersweet day for the Captain, because he and Lora had first met aboard the boat. He was the steward and she was a passenger in the early days when the *Nenana* was the glowing, pristine Queen of the

Yukon. He very much wished he could have shared her return to
grandeur with Lora.

Yet, Howard was not gloomy that day as he inspected and marveled
at our work. He praised the restoration while touring the boat in a new
uniform, identical to his original. He greeted scores of spectators,
answered questions, and reminisced with four of his officers who had
made the trip north to share the day with him. It was easy to see that,
to them, he would always be the Captain.

I was still with the Foundation in 1995 when Howard's sister, Elizabeth
Jarvi, and her daughter Rebecca Ferguson, made the trip from Seattle to
tour the *Nenana* and to present me with gifts that Howard had left.
Included were his captain's hat and jacket and pictures of himself and of
his uncle, Capt. Charles, both of them in their uniforms. And there were

seven hand-made copies of *A Cheechako Goes to the Klondike*, six of which immediately grew legs and disappeared!

Elizabeth also gave us two very large hardbound logbooks with sketches, the oldest dating to 1890, of Yukon River channel changes hand draw by a succession of riverboat captains. Capt. Charles Adams had bought them in 1901 for use with the *Lavelle Young*, added his own career drawings, and then passed them on to Howard to do the same.

Elizabeth and I agreed her uncle's story needed to be preserved because of its historic value to Fairbanks, insights into the business of operating steam-powered riverboats during the Klondike era, and a unique, richly detailed account of day-to-day life in the north.

For a time I looked for an underwriter and, finding none, decided to back publication myself through the John D. Williams Trust in joint venture with Epicenter Press Inc., a publisher of Alaska books founded in Fairbanks in 1988 and now located in the Seattle area.

Our intent is for this book to be the prototype for the Alaska Heritage Library, a series dedicated to the celebration of northern history through preservation of written accounts from an earlier time.

Every year in mid-July, the Fairbanks community engages in a ten-day celebration to commemorate the city's founding and to honor the founders. The streets are filled with sourdoughs and cheechakos as well as honorary sourdoughs and cheechakos, a.k.a. visitors and guests. Thousands of people are gussied up in remarkably imaginative and creative era costumes. They dance, sing, feast, parade, and eagerly join in the many activities that literally take over the community.

This year is special—the 100th birthday of the Golden Heart City and the 50th anniversary of Golden Days. This year will see a vibrant, soaring energy level that I am sure the first citizens would recognize and agree is not unlike that of Fairbanks in their time.

I am equally sure they would agree it is an ideal year for *A Cheechako Goes to the Klondike* to make its appearance.

Certainly, Charles Adams, the Barnettes, Felix Pedro, Dan McCarty, Frank Cleary, and Tom Gilmore would agree.

—Jack Williams, *Fairbanks, June 2002*

Introduction

Charles W. Adams is a good example of the few smart, ambitious, and tough men and women who followed the golden trail north at the turn of the century to seek their fortunes—and actually found them!

Even among this select group, Adams was unique. Following a common practice of the time, he kept a detailed record of his experiences and adventures, as did many others. The difference is that when a manuscript was developed from his journal, intended for publication as a book, the first-person narrative was retained, keeping it simple. Its story is neither embellished nor diluted, but rather clear, personal, and highly evocative.

With few exceptions, Adams was a positive thinker with a can-do attitude. When something went wrong, it was fixed. His goals were pursued to achievement without fanfare and replaced purposefully with new objectives.

To his family, he was an enigma. He did not have any children of his own. His nephew, Howard, and his niece, Elizabeth, describe Adams as strict but fair, active, quiet, shy around women, caring but not demonstrative, observant, and always in control of himself in any situation. He was devoted to his wife, Helen, and was profoundly saddened by her death in 1958.

By his own account, Adams was on his way home from business

school in Illinois to the family farm in North Dakota in 1897 when he heard about the Klondike Stampede. The next spring, he and three partners headed north by way of Seattle, traveling to the Klondike via Dawson and subsequently mining for gold in the Dawson area.

Although he was a successful miner, Adams recognized that there was money to be made providing services to the gold-seekers. In 1900, Adams purchased the *Lavelle Young* at St. Michael with two partners. The three men hired a captain and pilot, a first mate, and two engineers, signing themselves on as crew. The sale price was $20,000, and the trio of investors made a $10,000 down payment with Adams putting up most of the money. The prospects of making a profit were good. At that time, the standard passenger fare upriver to Dawson was $125, and freight was moved at $100 at ton.

Despite some early mechanical problems, the boat was used for a number of years for various purposes, mostly carrying cargo and people to settlements along the Yukon, and for what turned out to be the historically important run up the Tanana River to the future site of Fairbanks in 1901.

According to Jack Kutz, a marine consultant and authority on riverboat history, Adams not only worked on the *Lavelle Young* for a number of years, but also served on other vessels—between his prospecting and mining ventures—before taking tests and receiving his master's papers in 1909.

Adams was the first captain of the *Nenana*, which was built at the river town of Nenana in 1934 for the Alaska Railroad. He served as master until his retirement in 1940, when he was succeeded by his nephew Howard, who had come aboard as a cabin boy in 1934. Howard Adams served as master of the *Nenana* until her last run in 1954.

CHEECHAKO

Chapter one

Gold Strike

In the summer of 1897 on my way home from Quincy, Illinois, where I had attended a business college, our train stopped at a junction for an hour or so. There we had lunch and at the next table, two men were talking about going to the Klondike to a big gold strike.

I went on home to the farm in North Dakota, but I kept thinking of that gold strike.

Next winter I had a letter from brother George in Edenburg, North Dakota, telling me that Tom Morgan, a brother-in-law and Knute Anderson were going to the Klondike. George wanted me to go along and he would grubstake me. I was more than willing. So Tom, Knute and I met in Grand Forks, North Dakota, in late February, then boarded a train for Seattle.

Most prospectors bought their outfits in Seattle but we decided to buy ours in Juneau, Alaska.

We took passage on the "Cottage City" bound for Juneau. The trip was uneventful except that one foggy, dark night we sailed into a blind cove and ran aground. The bow of the ship stuck on the shore and was slightly damaged. The passengers got excited. One young man jumped overboard—then had to swim ashore. When daylight came, they were able to patch up the break in the bow, then back off when the tide came in, and go on to Juneau.

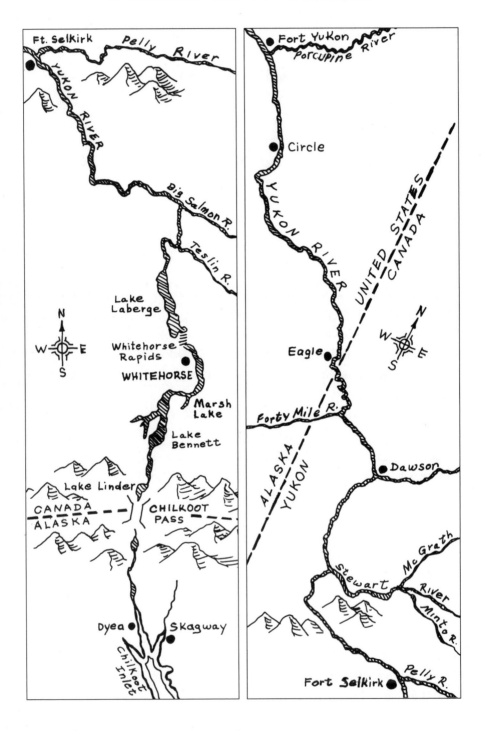

We were two days in Juneau buying our outfit which weighed 3,300 lbs. We heard that the Northwest Mounted Police would not let anyone go into Dawson country if they did not have 1,100 pounds of grub for each man. The bulk of our outfit was flour, beans, bacon and hardtack with the addition of sugar, rice and dried apricots. A salesman sold us a small quarter of dried salt beef which weighed 75 pounds. We also bought moccasins, woolen socks and blankets, mackinaw, trousers and coats which were very warm.

We boarded a small boat for Dyea which stopped first at Skagway to unload freight. While there, we went a short distance up the White Pass Trail. At one place we saw a man with a small table set up and he was manipulating three nut shells with a pea under one, while the stampede was going by. If bettors thought they could tell which shell the pea was under, they, of course, had to bet real money on their choice. When the gambler lifted the shell, the pea was never there. This was the notorious Soapy Smith Shell Game.

Finally the boat took us the short distance across the bay to Dyea and put our goods ashore. In our outfit we had three Yukon sleds, a Yukon stove, axes, a whipsaw, and other tools.

We commenced hauling our goods up the frozen Dyea River. It took us about four trips each to cover the few miles before we could make camp. By that time it was dark and we had a terrible time finding things. The tent was in a bundle by itself, and easy to find but not so easy to set up.

Knute cut a dry pole for the stove and some poles for the tent. Next he found some spruce boughs for us to sleep on. After a lot of trouble, I found the hardtack, bacon, tea and our cooking utensils, and was able to fry bacon, and make tea. We were very hungry by then and the bacon, hardtack and tea tasted mighty good.

Tom had the tent half up when it fell down on him so we just spread out blankets on the spruce boughs and pulled the tent over us and had a fine sleep.

The next morning, after a breakfast of bacon, tea and hardtack, we each took a small box on our sleds and started for Sheep Creek. On our way we met a freighter who had a large team of horses. He said he could take our whole outfit in one load so we hired him.

We made camp at Sheep Creek. Next morning each took a 65 lb. pack on his back and started the climb up Chilkoot Pass. There was a continuous line from daylight until dark. It was about a half-mile climb with steps cut in the snow all the way up. When a person became tired he could step out into a cut-out resting place, then back into line again.

After reaching the summit, you pulled your loads on the snow and started down. We just sat down and slid which took only about ten minutes. There were six or eight trenches about eight feet deep, worn down from the continuous sliding.

That night we decided it would take too long to get all our outfit up on our backs, so we hired the tram company which had started operating. We had an easy trip up to the summit without packs on our backs. Going down the other side was easy and we could take big loads on our sleighs. We had to sit in front of the sleigh with a snubbing stick to keep from going too fast. When everything was down we took small loads and went down six miles to Lake Linderman where we made camp. I stayed in camp a day and cooked a pot of beans and bacon which tasted mighty good. I also cooked some dried apricots. On the rest of our trip we had beans and bacon three times a day.

On the third day we began to feel burning sensations in our stomachs. Handfuls of snow which we ate did not help. An old timer told us we were eating too much bacon and. bacon grease and after eating less we were all right.

Three days later we heard the news that a big snow slide had occurred and buried Sheep Camp and don't know how many men were lost. If we had not been in such a hurry we might have been in it.

The morning after getting all our goods down to Linderman we started, each with a load of about 300 lbs., for Bennett, a town at the head of Lake Bennett. We went on down about nine miles and piled our loads ashore, then back to camp. This we did each day until we had moved everything. Then we would keep on past our cache for about fifteen miles and make camp again.

Knute was a coffee drinker and this time he was craving a cup of coffee. He went into an eating place in Bennett for a cup. They charged him 25 cents so he lost his craving for it after that. We had nothing but tea because coffee weighed too much. Knute was also a tobacco user but had none because it also weighed too much—and yet we had that 75 lb. chunk of dried salt beef that we could not eat. I tried stewing, boiling and roasting it but no good—so we threw it away.

Knute was talking to a man on the trail one day when the man took out a plug of tobacco and bit off a big chew. Well, Knute couldn't help asking him for a chew and the man refused him. It made Knute mad and in telling us about it he said that when he got to Dawson, he was going to buy a whole plug of tobacco and throw it in the river—and he did!

We finally got down to the foot of Lake Bennett which is about 28 miles long. Tom had a Smith & Wesson revolver. Knute had a 44 Colt and a Bowie knife. I had nothing but we had a 303 Savage rifle which we shared. Tom had set up a target two or three different places and had taken some practice shots with our rifle, so, he said, when he saw a moose he would be able to hit it.

Knute and I did not take any practice shots, but at home on the farm my brother Howard and I could hit a gopher or ground squirrel in the head with a 22 rifle every time—almost!

In camp one afternoon Tom shot six squirrels. They left me in camp and I cooked the squirrels. It was a big job to skin and clean them but I did. They made a fine tasting stew. I also cooked a pot of rice and made baking powder biscuits, so that night we had a great feast.

One morning while at our camp below Lake Bennett, a strong wind was blowing down stream so, like others were doing, we rigged up sails on our sleighs with some canvas we had. We were then able to each take 800 lbs. on our sleighs. The wind blew us all the way down and all we had to do was steer the sleigh with the gee poles. That was the only day the wind helped us.

The next lake below Bennett is Lake Tagish and then Lake Marsh. These lakes are about the same length as Bennett, and we kept on relaying our goods down each day until we reached the foot of Lake Marsh where the head of a river starts going down to the canyon. This river was open so we made camp and started to set up our canvas boat which would carry about three tons or more and three men. We got it set up and found it would only carry about 300 lbs. and two men. We started taking what we could as far as the head of the canyon and then had to tow the boat back, but we kept at it and finally got everything down.

CHEECHAKO

Chapter Two

Boating

We now knew, of course, that we would have to build a boat. We cut down large spruce trees, rigged up a swing place and went to work with our whipsaw. We had the logs up about six and one-half feet and I would be on top and Tom underneath. Knute was a good carpenter so he built the boat. It took us about ten days I guess.

One day after getting all the lumber sawed I thought I would make some yeast bread so got out some Magic Yeast cakes and went to work. I could only bake one small loaf at a time in our little Yukon stove but the bread was very good.

The boat was finally built and as we had no oakum or pitch, we had to cork the seams with torn up flour sacks and then gathered pitch from the spruce trees, melted it and then pitched the seams. It was a good sized boat, about 18 feet long and easily held everything.

We loaded up one morning and started down, tying up above the canyon. We walked down the rim and on down to the Whitehorse Rapids. The water there was certainly traveling—seemed to be going about thirty miles an hour with a big wave boiling up in the center. Lots of accidents had occurred in running these rapids and some lives were lost.

We and several others were watching the rapids and one old timer said you had to keep your boat right in the middle where the water looked the worst—otherwise your boat would hit the side walls and be wrecked.

We went back to our boat above the canyon and started down. Knute took the bow oar, I was in the center and Tom sat in the stern steering.

Once you entered the canyon, the water became very swift and no turning back. The thing to do was row as hard as you could so as to have steerage. Just after entering, Tom called to me saying there was something the matter with Knute. I glanced back and there sat poor Knute in a trance, eyes wide open, face green—and he had quit rowing. Well, I took his oar and then rowed with two oars, and I rowed as if our lives were at stake. We were able to keep in the center and in no time were through the canyon, then on through Squaw Rapids and on through the Whitehorse Rapids. Lucky we were to have had that man tell us to keep in the middle!

Floating below the rapids we saw something in the water and found it was a sack of flour from some boat that had been wrecked. It was only wet half of an inch deep so we were able to use most of it.

We floated on downstream to Lake Laberge, about 25 miles. You know, only a crazy person would *row* going downstream, only just to keep away from the river banks.

Lake Laberge was, of course, frozen over solid so we had to get our outfit, boat and all, out on the ice and commence hauling it down to an island twelve miles below where we made camp. Lake Laberge is the last of the lakes.

We loaded up each sled and started down to the foot of the lake, eighteen miles below. The snow was all melted from the top of the ice by this time, so we could take pretty big loads. But eighteen miles down and eighteen miles back was a lot of miles to make each day.

On our second day at the foot of the lake, I noticed a man who was starting back. He had a pole ten feet long sharpened at one end, and standing up on his empty sled he was poling along about three times faster than a person could walk. So I got a pole, sharpened one end and tried it. At first the sled would go out from under me and I would fall down but soon I was able to go along fine and got back to the camp two hours before Knute and Tom came along. I had eaten my supper, had theirs ready, and I was sound asleep when they came.

The next day Knute tried poling his sleigh back but after one fall, he threw the pole away and walked. Tom did not try it.

Soon came the day when we loaded the boat onto the sled and put everything aboard and started on our last trip. Thirty Mile River which empties Lake Laberge was, of course, open. All we had to do was to get the boat in open water, load everything and start downstream. Thirty Mile is a swift river but was like nothing after running the Canyon and Whitehorse.

The Hootalinqua River came in thirty miles below and then on down past the Big and Little Salmon Rivers. We ran into an ice jam and had to tie up for two days until the jam broke. Then we had clear sailing down through the Five Fingers Rapids. Farther down the Selkirk River comes in and we were stopped by another ice jam for a couple of days. We kept going, past the White River and on to the mouth of the Stewart River. Here we stopped—we had it figured out that all the ground would be staked around Dawson, 70 miles below, and that we would go up the Stewart River and find new ground.

Our boat was too large to tow upstream so we made a cache of it and most of our outfit. We took a small amount in our canvas boat and started up the river. We reached the mouth of the river on May 12.

The going was hard—very hard. That canvas boat was just like pulling a tub through the water. It took us four days towing, poling and rowing to make sixty miles or so. In one place we had stopped to rest and rearrange things in the boat. Knute picked up the axe and it dropped and fell blade down against the canvas bottom of the boat, cutting a hole in it. We got our things out in a hurry, but that was the end of Mr. Boat.

I have always thought that Knute did it on purpose, and I was very glad. Then we had to whipsaw lumber and build a poling boat— something we should have done at the mouth of the river.

We were lucky to be on a shore where there were a lot of nice large spruce trees. We made camp and Tom and I started cutting down trees and getting them ready to saw into lumber.

By this time prospectors were going by in poling boats and when some stopped to talk, we saw how a poling boat should be made. They, like ourselves, were all going upstream looking for gold, and all in a hurry.

Tom and I worked long and hard cutting the trees into lumber and then, while Knute was building the boat I had time to make more yeast bread. I made hot cakes three different mornings and made some syrup to go on them. How good they tasted! I had saved up a lot of bacon grease in empty tea cans and one day made some doughnuts. It was easy to make a rolling pin, but more difficult to make a cutter. I took a round piece of wood, tied short knives to it by the handles and it worked pretty good. The small hole I had to cut out with a jackknife. Anyway they tasted good, especially to Knute who was a doughnut and coffee lover, except that we had no coffee which bothered me none as we never had coffee at home anyway.

There was a high mountain some distance back of us and I took our rifle one morning and set out to climb it and what a climb it was—much higher than I thought—and near the top it became very steep. I got on top though, and what a view—and something else, too—a flock of mountain sheep. Out of that herd came a big old ram with his head down and traveling about sixty miles an hour. I was scared stiff—but not so stiff that I couldn't turn and run like I had never run before, and Mr. Ram gave up the chase. Me, I kept on going—I had no desire to see what was up there at all.

That night in camp they asked why I had not taken a shot at the ram and I told them I was getting out of there too fast to stop and take a shot at anything!

The boat was finally finished but we found, after launching it, that the sides were too straight. It would tip over very easily. All we had to do was to bend the sides out and keep them out with a short ship brace. Then we loaded up and started upstream.

CHEECHAKO

Chapter three

McQuesten River

Word came now from boats going by that there had been a gold strike on the McQuesten River some forty miles above.

With our new boat, we could get along like anybody else. While building our poling boat, a man came drifting down on a raft. He stopped and we gave him our canvas boat. He thought he could stop the leak. He was on the way to Dawson, had quarreled with his partners and left them.

On our second day we were towing the boat along as we had a nice beach for some distance. We saw a piece of driftwood above us and across the river. It had something sticking up from it. When I happened to look again, it was halfway across the river, and we saw it was not a piece of driftwood, but a bull moose, with hip, head and horns out of water. We immediately stopped because it would land about 150 feet above us. It was then Tom did a peculiar thing. He got the rifle out of the boat and gave it to me. I took the rifle and when the moose reached shallow water, he commenced to walk. I should have waited until he was out of the water, but I didn't, I shot when he was only partly out and I hit him just back of the shoulder. He dropped, but thrashed around some and got into deep water. He started floating down stream with just his horns sticking out of water. I got in the boat, telling them to shove it out, and as the moose came by I took hold of its horns and they pulled us ashore.

Well, we had a big bull moose and did not quite know what to do with him. It was then a boat came along with a party of four prospectors and they helped us to get the moose up on higher ground. Luckily one of these men was a butcher from Kansas City and he proceeded to cut up the moose. We all took what we wanted; the rest we put on a pole bench we made, with a sign on it saying, "Help yourself." Later we heard that every bit of that moose was used up.

The next night we had moose steaks and you can imagine how good they tasted after having no fresh meat for several months.

We soon reached the mouth of the McQuesten River and a stampede was going on to a creek up the river some distance. We camped there at the mouth of the McQuesten River and made ready to go on the stampede the next morning. That night we heard something moving around our tent and on looking out saw another big bull moose. It heard us and moved away into the woods.

Next morning we took packs on our backs, along with a blanket and some hardtack and bacon. There was no trail, of course; just had to keep going as best we could along the creek. We camped that night, all tired out, and in the morning while eating breakfast, we heard something moving at the creek about thirty feet away. A moose had come to drink. Knute grabbed his revolver and shot at it. The moose raised up its head to see what was going on and then Tom shot at it with his revolver. The poor moose turned around and went off into the woods. Knute was so excited that he did not know that Tom had fired a shot also and we never told him.

That afternoon, while going along, we caught up with several more stampeders and as we did not seem to get to the creek where the gold find was, we finally figured we were going up a creek which emptied into the main stream a few miles from the mouth. We started across country and that evening arrived at the right place. I have forgotten the name of the creek, but anyway we were too late. It was all staked from one end to the other. There must have been 100 men or more.

Nothing to do next morning but go back to camp and start upstream again. The Mayo River comes in about 20 or 30 miles, I think, above the McQuesten. Two days above the Mayo we were joined by two other men.

From then on we kind of traveled together and camped in the same place at night. One of the men was planning to bake a loaf of bread in the ashes and coals of a camp fire. It was sourdough bread, baked in a gold pan and a second gold pan to cover it.

He gave me a starter of sourdough in an empty screw top tea can. The weather was quite warm now and the next afternoon we heard an explosion and found out that the sourdough had exploded and everything in the boat was sprayed with sourdough—quite a mess!

The river was high and still coming up. One night it flooded our camp. We awakened in time and got to higher ground in a hurry.

The next night another boat with three men came along at camping time. In talking with one of those three, Knute and he decided they did not want to go any farther. So next morning they stayed, taking their share of our outfits. They built a raft and floated down to Dawson.

Now there were three boats, with two men in a boat. The following day we reached the Stewart River Falls, which are about thirty feet high, and the water drops straight down. We had no choice but to pack everything up and around the falls. Then the six of us could lift and move each boat around and above the falls. In another day or so we came to another rapids but could easily pull the boats through with the tow lines. Then another day's journey we came to a long canyon. In the lower part we were able to tow the boats along, but the upper part was too swift. Then we got all our tow lines and ropes together. Five men climbed out and up to the head of the canyon taking the ropes along. After tying all these ropes together, they tied one end to a large piece of driftwood and shoved it down river. They had left me with the three boats tied together, one behind the other.

I was in the first boat, the others tied behind, and I caught the driftwood as it came along. Then I tied it to the boat I was in, cast loose from shore, and after jerking the rope several times as a signal, they pulled me and the three boats up and out of the canyon. All I had to do was keep the boats from going against the bank or shore.

After we were camped for the evening I walked around in the woods and came across a big bull moose that someone had shot and killed just so they could brag about killing a moose.

CHEECHAKO

Chapter four

Dawson

In camp one evening we got to talking about why we were going upriver as none of us were doing any prospecting, just going along, working hard each day for nothing, and right then we all decided to go back. Next morning we started downstream, letting the current in the river do the work.

We stayed together until we got the boats below the Stewart River Falls, then parted. The trip down stream was easy and uneventful. At the mouth we stopped and took aboard our outfit which we had cached, and then on to Dawson, seventy miles below.

Arriving in Dawson we camped in a place called Lousetown, just across the Klondike River above Dawson.

While putting up the tent, a man came along and offered to help us. We asked him to stay for dinner. He did and stayed with us for a long time. His name was James Gill.

Since the time we first arrived at Dyea and climbed to Chilkoot, none of us had ever shaved. Our beards were six inches long, more or less. Tom and I went over to Dawson for a shave and a haircut. Our smooth-shaven faces seemed to look so funny afterwards.

The next day, while walking around Dawson, we saw a woman with a little girl about the same age as Tom's little girl back home. It made Tom feel so lonesome that he decided to go home. He bought a ticket on a passenger river steamboat and left Dawson next day.

Over in Dawson one day I met a man I had known back home. He told me that he and three other men were going on the following day to stake some claims they had heard about on a hillside up on Hanker Creek, and I could go along. Next morning I met them and we went up the creek which flows into the Klondike some miles above Dawson.

They had a map and we found the hillside and the place to stake the claims, which we did. We came back to Dawson on the following day and went to the recording office to record them. The recording clerk told us that those claims had already been recorded. We were foolish and let the matter drop. Later those claims proved to be good and that clerk turned out to be a crook. He told some of his friends who went up and staked them. The department got after him for that and other things, and he had to leave the country. He hid out on a passenger boat going down river and did not show up until below Eagle on the way to St. Michael.

About a week later I went on a stampede to the lower part of Gold Run Creek. Jim was working in a sawmill by this time.

Several of us went up Bonanza Creek to the head of the creek and on up on the edge, along it and finally down to Gold Run and into the lower part. It was almost dark now and we found we were too late—ground was all staked. It was quite a disappointment but nothing could be done about it. Some of us knew who had started this stampede anyway. I had no blankets and nothing to eat except some hardtack and cold fried bacon. The others all had blankets and could sleep. With none, I could not sleep so I started back at the first sign of daylight.

Late in the afternoon I reached a point a short distance below Grand Forks and had stopped to rest. I was very tired by this time. A man came out of his tent near where I was sitting and he said to me, "You look very tired, young man. Where have you been?"

After telling him, he said, "No wonder you are tired and I'll bet hungry also. I am going to get something to eat and then going to work. I'm on the night shift on the claim just below so after I eat, you help yourself and then go into my tent and turn in."

He said he would not be in until six next morning. I was very hungry and tired. He had the usual pot of bacon and beans and they were so very good; also there was the usual pot of tea. Then I went into the tent and into his bunk; and fell asleep immediately. I never awakened until six next morning when he got off shift. We had breakfast and after thanking him, I was on my way. That man and his kindness has always remained a bright spot in my life to think about.

CHEECHAKO

Chapter five

Moose-Hunting

Now it was getting near the last of August and Jim and I thought we would go moose hunting; get a moose, bring it to Dawson and sell it. We started one morning, each with a pack of about fifty pounds. We had to have blankets, hardtack, tea and bacon, an axe and our rifles.

At the end of the second day we thought we were about thirty miles from Dawson. We thought that the other side looked better for hunting than the side we were on. I guess we were like the moose and caribou; every time they come to a river they swim across.

The Klondike River is not a large river, but quite swift and in some of the swift places, not very deep. I got a six-foot pole and started to cross the river. It was really a foolish thing to do—crossing that swift river with a pack on my back and carrying a rifle. A person could easily slip on a stone or something and then it would be too bad. I made it, though, and called to Jim to come. He started, but being shorter than I, the water came further up on him. After a few feet, he went back. Then he had to go upstream a short distance to find two or three drift logs, tie them together into a raft and come across.

I had built a fire and was pretty well dried out when Jim got across. While he was drying out, we talked of what to do next. Jim said that an old time hunter back in Idaho where he came from said the best and easiest way was to find an old animal trail and just sit there and wait for the game to come along. When he was getting his raft logs, he said he thought he saw where a creek came into the river. We went up there and up the creek a few miles where we made camp; then set out to perhaps find an animal trail.

Quite a distance up the creek we did find what appeared to be a trail. Then we found a well hidden spot where one of us could keep watch.

It was now about six in the afternoon, we thought I should keep the first watch until midnight, so Jim went back to camp and I sat down to wait for something to come along. I hoped it would be a large bull moose. Nothing came—but Jim at midnight! Our camp was about two miles below. We kept that up for three days but we saw only rabbits and one day a large black bear.

We were getting quite discouraged. On the fourth day, early in the morning, I was in camp when Jim came along and his first words were, "I told you so; I shot a moose."

We had breakfast and then went up there. Sure enough he had shot our moose—a big bull moose. After dressing it, the big question was how to get it down to the river. You know, a large moose weighs several hundred pounds.

Well, we dragged and rolled it to the creek which was only about twenty yards. We then made a raft and, while the water was not deep enough to float it, we could, by walking along each side and lifting it along, bump slowly down to the river.

There we made a large raft that would carry Mr. Moose and us too and got started down the river. We each had a pole. All we had to do was keep the raft away from the shores. We figured the river current took us along about seven miles an hour. At that time fresh meat was very scarce in Dawson and brought a good price, especially moose killed in the latter part of August.

We reached Dawson late in the evening and next morning went to a restaurant. We saw the proprietor and told him what we had. He immediately came along to our raft, took one look and then offered us five hundred dollars for it—just as it was—hide, horns and all. We thought that fair enough and so sold it to him. He paid us in gold dust—buying and selling was all done in gold dust in Dawson at that time.

We were idle for a few days. Sometimes in the evening we would walk around Dawson and go into the saloons and dancehalls and gambling places. I did not dance and had never tasted any kind of liquor or gambled. I was very bashful—so bashful that it has been a handicap to me all my life. If, while watching the girls dance, one of them had come and spoken to me, I would have fainted.

One day the sawmill owner came to our tent and asked us if we would work in the sawmill a few days. We agreed and worked for him fifteen days. Then he shut down as he had all his logs sawed up. He paid us ten dollars a day—one dollar an hour which was good wages in those days.

CHEECHAKO

Chapter six

Winter

It was late September and time to get settled for the winter. Someone told us about a creek sixteen miles above Dawson that no one had prospected as yet. So we got some of our outfit together and into the poling boat.

We found the creek all right and found a nice place for a cabin three miles up from the mouth so went to work building. There were quite a number of spruce trees there. It took us about a week to build the cabin. We put moss between the logs. We made a pole roof with the moss and dirt on the poles. We took our boat to pieces, using the lumber to make a door and table and two bunks. That cabin was certainly snug and warm.

We started to sink a shaft near the creek to look for gold. Bedrock was only about twenty feet down, but it was slow work. We had to thaw the ground and on reaching bedrock, we found nothing.

We had one small window in the cabin—but had no glass. We put a piece of a towel over it, and one morning saw something poking at our window. We went outside quietly and there was a martin poking around. On seeing us, it ran away. We got the idea that we would try to do some trapping. The trouble was we had no traps.

Jim's hunting friend back in his home town told him how to make a figure-four trap so Jim was going to try. We had not brought everything up from Dawson—the poling boat would not carry everything. We had left 300 pounds of flour and the two sleds. As the river was now frozen over, it being about the middle of October, I started for Dawson early one morning.

Jim had seen signs of caribou some distance away and was going to try to get one. We needed some fresh meat.

There was a kind of trail on the river ice down to Dawson on the other side and I made the sixteen miles easy enough, got the flour and one load and started back. It had started to snow and my sleigh became harder and harder to pull. I had to stop and rest very often. Finally it became dark and I was all in. I was within a few miles of our creek when I had to leave the sleigh.

I could hardly make it to the mouth of our creek, sat down and rested awhile—then on again, but sitting down more often. It got so that when I sat down I would go to sleep and always dreamed that a big black wolf was coming at me and I would awaken, get up and stagger on. Guess it was a good thing for that big black wolf to wake me up each time as the weather was cold now.

I finally did reach our cabin and fell down against the door. Jim heard me and dragged me inside. After I had slept awhile, he gave me some tea and something to eat. I then slept until about eight the next morning and after a good breakfast, was all right. Jim had shot a young caribou and the meat was wonderful.

I had an idea that I could make a trap out of an empty 5-gallon can. I got to work opening one and completely nailed strips along two sides, then cut a one-inch slot across the top so that a one-inch thick door would slide up and down. I fixed a nail with a string to it which would keep the door up and the string to the back and down into the can. I tied a dead camp-robber bird to the string. A camp-robber bird is about the size of a robin.

I figured that Mr. Martin would go in to get the bait and when he did he would pull the nail out that was holding the door up and down would come the door. I had a nail placed so it slid down and stopped the door from going up again. I set my trap out in the evening close to the cabin and caught a martin in a few hours. We could hear him trying to get out of the can but he was caught and no way out.

I set the trap around in different places. Finally, I was setting it eight miles or so from the cabin and I caught a martin almost every night. Jim had very little success with his trap but did get a fox.

One day I shot a porcupine. They are good eating but this one was very fat. It was an old one, I guess. Later on Jim got a young one and it was fine—just like chicken.

CHEECHAKO

Chapter seven

Lonesome

Along about the first of November, I became restless and lonesome for the home folks, so I decided to start for the outside. A lot of people were going out over the ice by this time—men like myself who had found no gold. Now the trail was good.

I did not have a sleeping bag and got the brilliant idea that I could make one out of canvas, so I soon had one made. One morning I loaded onto one of the sleighs some bacon, beans, hardtack, a teapot and tea, my blanket and sleeping bag—said goodbye to Jim and was on my way.

I made about twenty-five miles that first day and at dark stopped for the night. I went into the woods, cut down a dry tree, and started a fire so I could fry bacon and make tea—and keep warm. It was 48° below zero.

After supper I sat close to the fire for awhile and pretty soon felt one of my moccasins getting tight on my foot. I drew my foot away from the fire and found I had burned a hole in one moccasin. I had an extra pair of moccasins so put on a good one. I sat down again and, believe it or not, I burned another moccasin! Now that I had only one pair I was very careful not to get my feet too near the fire again.

Then it was time to try out my sleeping bag. I had already fixed my blanket in it, and having placed some spruce boughs on the snow, I put the bag on them and crawled in. I was in that bag about five minutes when I knew I would freeze to death in no time; so for the rest of the night I sat by the camp fire, being very careful not to get my feet too close. I was so glad when it began to get daylight. I had tea, hardtack and bacon and was on my way. About an hour before dark that day I came to a roadhouse for the night. There were eight or ten guests there that night.

The owner came to me and asked me if I would help him. He did not have enough firewood cut up. I took his axe out, saw a dry tree and went to work. Soon I had sawed and cut up quite a pile of stove wood. In a little while the owner told me I had more than enough. For dinner that evening we had moose steak, bacon and beans and sourdough bread which was very good.

Then we sat around talking and telling hunting stories. I told them about an incident that occurred when we were on our trip up the Stewart River. We had stopped one noon for lunch, and another boat had stopped with us with two men in it. At this point a slough came into the river. While eating we heard a noise and looking up we saw a cow moose with her calf that had entered the slough and were swimming across. Knute grabbed our rifle and one of the other men got his rifle. As the moose started to climb up the bank, Knute said to the other brave hunter, "Which do you want the cow or the calf?"

He was too excited to answer. They both commenced shooting and the moose climbed on up the bank and into the woods. They were sure they had hit the moose so we went over and looked for an hour or so—but no sign of them. I laugh every time I think of Knute saying, "Which do you want—the cow or the calf?"

We had nice warm bunks to sleep in at the roadhouse that night and after a breakfast of sourdough hot cakes and moose stew, we got ready to leave. When I offered to pay my bill, the roadhouse man said I owed him nothing. He said he was in debt to me if anything for all that wood I had cut up.

On the trail that day I caught up with two other men. We became acquainted and they said as long as I had no tent, I could camp with them, which I was glad to do. I helped put the tent up that evening, got spruce boughs and laid down to sleep on them. We each had a blanket and after putting canvas on the boughs, we put one blanket under us and two on top. They also told me to sleep in the middle so I was plenty warm. They had a small Yukon stove. In cooking supper the tent became nice and warm, but it was still 40° or 50° below outside.

The next afternoon we arrived at the mouth of the Stewart River where there was a roadhouse. We stayed in the roadhouse all night.

One of the new companions of mine was Herman Mueller and he and I hit it off well together. He had a basket sleigh and the other man an open sleigh like mine. Next morning Herman and I decided to put our things together on his basket sleigh, and in rearranging our sleds we had to leave a bag of salt and some flour.

Herman's sleigh had handles at the back so a man could walk along at the back and push on the handles. We started out with me ahead pulling the sleigh and Herman behind pushing. After an hour or so we would change off. Then Sam, the other man, wanted to change with us, so he got behind our sleigh. The trouble was that he would just walk along and not shove it. If anything, he would ride on the handles. So pretty soon Herman and I would not change off with him. He was a shirker; would let us do all the camp work.

We always stopped long enough before dark to make camp. It is very difficult to make camp in the dark but no trouble at all to break camp in the dark, so we could start out as early as we liked.

In a few more days we were going along at the foot of a big bluff where the wind had blown the snow off the ice and I slipped and fell. In doing so, I put my right thumb out of joint. I showed it to Herman. He grabbed it, gave a jerk and pulled it back into place.

That day we reached Selkirk. It was too early to stop so we went on to Five Finger Rapids where we camped for the night. All this time it had been very cold—40° to 50° below zero. But this night at Five Fingers, I happened to wake up near morning and heard the wind blowing and knew we would have warmer weather.

When we got up we found it was quite warm. A warm Chinook wind was blowing from the southwest. By noon the snow commenced to melt and soon there was water on the trail. We tried to dodge around it at first but soon just walked along in the water in our moccasin-clad feet.

In camp that night we found our flour and hardtack had become wet. All the provisions we had left were some cornmeal and a little bacon and tea. So it was cornmeal mush without salt and a little bacon for supper. I made a campfire and sat there to dry out my socks and moccasins.

The next morning we had a little mush without salt and a little bacon and on again. We had one more wet day on the ice, then it turned cold that night and froze solid again. Two or three days more and we reached the foot of Lake Laberge where there was a roadhouse where we stayed all night. We had a good dinner that evening—Lake Laberge Whitefish—and how we did eat. I thought we would never get enough.

In the morning the proprietor sold us some bacon and beans and a nice large whitefish so on we went. We camped that night at the head of the lake and next day made it to Whitehorse and on up to the head of the canyon where we made camp. There we were able to buy supplies at a kind of roadhouse—a little bacon, some hardtack, also some rice and a few raisins. I put a pot of rice and raisins on to cook and after eating hardtack and bacon, we started on the rice. We kept on eating until it was all eaten. We did not seem to be able to get enough to eat.

There was now a new road from the head of the canyon to the foot of Lake Bennett. We made the foot of that lake by nightfall and found the lake had not frozen over yet so next morning we left our sleighs and almost everything. We each had a pair of light leather shoes. We put them on and started up the bank of the lake. It was very hard walking, some places over rocks, but we did reach Bennett, the town at the lake's head, and stayed in a roadhouse all night. Next day up early and on over the White Pass reaching Skagway late that evening. I think the distance from Dawson to Skagway is 400 miles, and in all of that trip none of us ever had a cold or became ill in any way, but the next day after reaching Skagway, we all had caught cold. It was now early December and I had been about twenty days or a little more on the trip.

A ship arrived in a few days and we took passage for Seattle. Reaching there, I hunted up a fur store, and sold my ten martin skins which I had brought along, getting eight dollars a skin for them.

Herman and I planned to come back the next spring and take a scow load of goods into Dawson including a lot of fresh fruit and vegetables. In a few days we boarded a Great Northern train for our homes. I would get off at Grand Forks, North Dakota, and then up to my home on the farm eighty miles north. He would go on to his home in Milwaukee, Wisconsin.

Leaving my train at Bathgate, North Dakota, I walked the seven miles out to our farm, stopping on the way at a farm to see a sister of mine, Mrs. Isa Renwick. They were surprised to see me as I had never written to anyone after I got started for the Klondike. I went on over home, a short distance. My mother and brother Howard were also surprised and pleased to see me.

CHEECHAKO

Chapter eight

North Dakota

There is not much to do on a farm in the winter in North Dakota, and time seemed to go slow. But the time did come to start back. I had gone to see my brother George, and he thought it a good idea for me to go back with Herman Mueller, and was willing to stake me again. About the middle of March we met in Seattle and then went over to Victoria, British Columbia. We figured that by buying our goods there, we would need to pay no duty on entering Canada. Dawson is in the Yukon Territory in Canada.

We bought fifteen tons of goods, oranges, lemons, apples, potatoes, eggs and a lot of other supplies; and lumber enough to build a scow. We also bought a small horse.

About the middle of March we took our goods and boarded a steamship bound for Skagway and Dyea. On arriving at Skagway, we took our horse ashore. The horse was taken over the White Pass to Bennett—we thought it the best Pass for a horse to go over. We went on over to Dyea and had all our goods taken up over Chilkoot by the Tram Company and down the other side. From there we would take them down to Bennett with our horse and sleigh. We, of course, walked over to Bennett. The horse arrived in Bennett the day after we did.

At this time there was a good trail from Bennett to this side of Chilkoot where our goods had been delivered. Next morning I led the horse up there, found our sleigh, and hitched up the horse. We loaded on our tent, company supplies and everything I thought we would need first when we went back to Bennett. We set up the tent for ourselves— also had a tent for the horse and a good blanket for him.

We had it all figured out. I was to get the supplies down and Herman's job was to build the scow. I brought a load of lumber down. Then I rode up on the empty sleigh and walked all the way back. We had our perishable goods stored in Skagway until the weather would be mild enough to bring them over.

After quite a while I had our goods all down. Then I walked over to Skagway and had our perishable goods shipped to Dyea and over to Chilkoot—and I started hauling them down. It was now getting warm and the trail was getting bad—got so the horse and sleigh would break through and I had a lot of trouble getting a load down. There was a freighting company in Bennett and we hired them to bring down the rest—just in the nick of time before the trail went all to pieces.

Herman had the scow nearly built. In a week or so we finished it, launched it in the lake one day and we started to load it. The lake was still frozen over so nothing to do but wait—along with a lot of others.

Finally the lake opened up. We loaded our scow with everything but the horse. We sold him to a couple of men who were taking a scow load of horses to Dawson.

We had a canvas sail on the scow and it did not take long to go down to the head of Lake Tagish which was not yet open so there was nothing to do but tie up and wait again.

Two men in a small boat tied up close to us and we soon became acquainted with them. One was a photographer from Chicago who came to Dawson the year before. He had a claim on Gold Hill which he to a leased to a man and he was going in now to see about it. When Lake Tagish finally opened, we told these two men to tie their boat to our scow. There was lots of room and they would not need to go ashore to sleep. We got down to Tagish and most of Lake Marsh but found the lower end still closed with ice. Soon there were a lot of scows and boats around waiting for the ice to clear up.

Tied up next to us was a scow and aboard it quite a number of vaudeville and dancehall girls. I think a man named Pantages was taking them to Dawson.

My partner, Herman, was not bashful like myself. He soon started talking to them. When they found out we had fresh fruit and eggs, they came aboard and bought a lot. One of the girls came over to where I was standing at one side near the edge of the scow. I started to back away from her, caught my heels on the two-inch corning and fell into the lake. They fished me out but, oh, the water was cold! I got one of the men to hold up a blanket while I got on my clothes. The girls had a great laugh. One of them said that if all the men in Dawson were like me, it was no use for them to go there.

The ice cleared away in a few more days so we could start again. We had no trouble running the canyon and Whitehorse Rapids. We both knew that we just had to keep in the center. We went on down to Lake Laberge which was open, with nothing to stop us now all the way to Dawson.

CHEECHAKO

Chapter nine

A Claim

Our photographer's partner went out on the creeks and the photographer stayed with us. Herman took charge of selling our supplies. He was a good salesman. I did the cooking and sorting things over. Our photographer's name was Henry. He went up to his claim one day and came back rather discouraged. His was a hillside claim and they had driven in a tunnel 200 feet or so looking for the paystreak. This tunnel was not logged up, so when the warm spring weather came, some of the roof and sides thawed out and dropped down filling the tunnel about three feet with gravel. He could not do any panning to see if they had found anything or not.

The next day after Henry had been up there, Olsen came down. He was the man to whom Henry had given the lease. He and Henry sat and talked while I was doing some cooking. I could hear everything that was said.

Olsen told Henry that he had hired men to help him drive in the main tunnel and hired some others. They had found nothing. He said Henry owed him several hundred dollars to help pay for all that work. He was willing to buy the claim from Henry. The next fall when cold weather came again, he could clean out the tunnel and prospect some more.

After the Swede left, poor Henry was very much discouraged. He told Herman and me all about it that evening. Next day when Herman and I were alone for awhile, I told Herman that the Swede was lying like hell. I said that is a good claim and we had better buy it.

Herman did not think much of the idea but finally agreed. Henry had taken a dislike to the Swede. That evening he told us he did not want to sell to the Swede but would sell it to us and go back to Chicago and home to his family. In a day or two the Swede came around again and when he heard that we had bought the claim, he was very much displeased.

Neither Herman nor I had ever been up where the claim was, and we knew nothing about mining. But I felt sure it was all right after I saw how the Swede acted when he heard we had bought it.

Herman soon sold all our goods at a good profit. We had more than enough to pay for the claim.

A few days later we went up to see what we had purchased. It was sixteen miles up Bonanza Creek and on what was called Gold Hill. Herman and I had each taken a pack on our backs with some grub and a couple of blankets. We talked to some other claim owners there who told us our claim could only be worked in the winter when the tunnel would be frozen. They said the tunnel could not be cleaned out until fall when the freezing weather came.

They also told us we would need 100 cords of wood to thaw the ground as we worked the claim. There was a creek a few miles below where we could cut the wood, so Herman and I went down there. The creek was called Adams Creek. This creek had been burned over and there was a lot of dry timber on it. The trouble was the wood had to be cut and then hauled to our claim.

By this time it was about the middle of June and quite warm. The mosquitoes were also very numerous and hungry. In fact, there could have been no more of them unless they had been a lot smaller. Herman did not like mosquitoes or the thought of cutting 100 cords of wood while the "little dears" were cutting into him. Another thing Herman did not like was the thought of packing grub and things up the sixteen miles to the claim from Dawson. We went down to Dawson next day and he told me he would like to sell his interest in the claim. I bought him out and when I paid him I had $7.50 left and some grub. I should have known better because now I was getting to be an old man—25 years old! Herman was going out to Vancouver to buy and bring in another scow load of goods.

For five days I packed a load on my back up to the claim—my blanket, grub, flour, bacon, beans and things, also our little Yukon stove which was not very heavy. There I was with $7.50 and a little grub and 100 cords of wood to cut.

I looked for and finally found a man, Tom McLain, who was willing to work on bedrock. That was the way most transactions were made. You hired men or bought things on bedrock, that is, when you got to bedrock and taking out gold, you would pay.

Tom and I each took a pack of grub, mostly bacon and beans, a small tent, and a crosscut saw and went to where we were to cut that 100 cords of wood.

We were to cut in sixteen foot lengths. We worked and the mosquitoes were not idle either. After many days we figured we had a little over 100 cords.

One day Tom cut down a tree that was hollow at the top. In it was a bees' nest and quite a lot of honey which we carefully gathered up. It was very wonderful when we put it on our bread and hot cakes.

It was getting late in the season. We figured when snow came we would hire a horse and sleigh to haul our wood to the claim. We would need hay for the horse, so we set to work, each with a butcher knife. There was lots of tall grass on the hillside. We would take large handfuls, cut it off and spread them out to dry. After drying, we tied the hay up in bundles with the hay shaft, then made a stack, and figured we had three tons.

It was late summer and nothing to do but wait until snow came, so we could haul the wood to the claim, and start cleaning out the tunnel. We did pack up a little more grub from Dawson.

The snow did finally come and I found while I could not hire a horse, I could get it hauled on bedrock by a man with a team of horses and a bob sleigh. He bought our hay, paying us $100 a ton. That grass was called Red Top and grew thick and high. Tom, or "Kentuck" as we called him, got tired waiting and went to work in another mine.

I hired a man after the first load of wood came. Kentuck and I had already cleaned out the tunnel. We built a fire in the back of the tunnel one evening to thaw the ground so we could prospect it. When we tried to go in next morning there was so much gas in the tunnel we could not go in. It only cleared out late in the afternoon.

I soon saw that I would have to get a steam boiler to thaw the ground. I went to Dawson to look for one and found a place where they made small steam pipe boilers. They cost a lot of money and they would not sell to me on bedrock.

I went back to the claim, not knowing what to do. Next day a neighbor told me he knew a grand fellow on the other end of the Hill who might put up the money. He was mining and doing very well. I went to see this man, Jim Clark, and he came over to my claim. After looking around, he said he would buy a half interest in my claim, and buy the boiler, and all other things needed, such as wheelbarrows to wheel the dirt out and shovels, picks, anything else needed. Everything cost a lot in those days.

We completed the deal and soon had a boiler brought up. It cost a lot to have it brought up. In addition we had to have a lot of steam pipe and thawing points. it seemed there was no end to what we needed. We did get everything ready, hired four men and started to work. We got steam up and drove the thawing points in at the far end of the tunnel one afternoon, then put a man on all night to keep steam up and watch the points. We could now thaw the ground without having any gas. In the daytime we could take out the thawed dirt, panning once in a while to see if there was any gold.

I think it was about the third day that we got some gold prospects and soon after hit real pay dirt. After a few days we set up a rocker in the tunnel, and sorting out the best pay dirt soon had a lot of gold dust. One day the apron on the rocker would fill up and we would have to stop rocking and scoop the gold out with a spoon. I soon had quite a few one pound tea cans filled and hid in the dirt floor of the boiler house. If that

Swede had drifted about six feet further, he would have found the good pay dirt.

The man we had on at night would pick up nuggets at the place where the points were thawing, giving them to us the next day.

We decided that I had better go on at night myself.

On those long nights I would pan out a panful of dirt once in a while and soon got good pans. In the morning I would show Jim, my partner, what I had and then he would try to beat me. The pay dirt kept getting richer and soon we were getting $70 and $100 pans. One day in taking out the thaw, we found a good sized quartz boulder or rock which was lying right on bedrock. Behind it the gold was lying as if it had been spilled there. Jim scooped it up into a pan and had $422. Well, I quit panning—I knew could never beat that.

Our paystreak was right next to bedrock, the good pay only about a foot or eighteen inches above bedrock. We only took out about three feet. All this pay dirt was taken with wheel barrows out on the dump. We paid our three men one dollar an hour and they had to board themselves. They stayed with me in the cabin. We all took turns at cooking. The main thing was, of course, bacon and beans. We worked ten hours a day.

CHEECHAKO

Chapter Ten

Gold

There was a town now near the foot of our hill, Grand Forks, on Bonanza Creek, and just above Eldorado Creek came in. I went down to Grand Forks one day for some things we needed. I bought four cans of strawberries, one for each of us. None of us had eaten anything like that for a long time and they were so good that we each ate a can at our dinner that evening. I paid five dollars for the four cans of strawberries.

One of our men had a bad toothache for a couple of days. He went down to the Forks to a dentist who said it should come out. Our man had it pulled and when he got back to the cabin he was boiling mad. Said the dentist had pulled the wrong tooth and he did not notice it until he was almost back. After a couple of days he went down and had the right one out.

There was no way to get water on the hill but by melting snow. Then it tasted of creosote, there was so much smoke around from thawing the ground out. About this time, February, I had a backache most of the time. Some said it was from using snow water and eating so much baking powder bread. I went down to Dawson to see a doctor. The one I went to had a small hospital there. He said it was nothing serious but to stay in the hospital a few days, which I did.

The way I was dressed, I looked just like any ordinary shovel stiff working in the mines, and the doctor was going to have me well in about four days. On the third day Jim, my partner, came to see me. He was on the showy side. He saw the doctor and they talked for some time. After Jim left, the doctor examined me and said my case was more serious than he had thought and I would need to be in the hospital a lot longer. The next day he lanced my back over the kidneys and drew the blood out by putting some alcohol in a glass, setting it afire, then turning it upside down over the lanced places. Rather rough treatment—but that was his way of drawing out blood and I have the scars on my back to this day to prove it.

There was a nurse in the hospital that I got to like very much, a Miss Hanna. I took her out to dinner a couple of times. One day she came to me and told me to get up and go home. She said there was nothing wrong with me. I went to see the doctor to pay my bill and, can you believe it, he borrowed $200 from me!

I thought I was in love with Miss Hanna, but did not have the nerve to tell her so. I kept thinking about it after I got back to the claim. Finally I wrote to her asking her to marry me. She did not answer the letter and when I could stand it no longer, I went down to Dawson to see her and took her out to dinner. After dinner I asked her if she had received my letter. She said she had. She told me that she was much too old for me and to forget about it, which I did in a few weeks.

Spring came at last and we had worked out all the good pay dirt from our claim. It was not a large claim, the back part had pay dirt. When the dirt we were taking out got to having only fifteen cents to the pan, we would not bother with it.

Along about the first of June we got ready to sluice up our dump. We had to rent a little steam boiler and pump down at the creek at the foot of the hill and ran a one inch pipe up to our sluice boiler.

We also had to get a pulsometer pump to pump the sluice water over and over, feeding it with the pump down at the creek. We had a rock box. I put on pair of gum boots and stood in it. With an eight-tined fork I would throw all the coarse stones out. One day I happened to notice that I had thrown out a nugget that was too large to go through the tines of the fork. You should have seen how quick I was about jumping down to pick it up!

We had to shut down one day to have one of the pumps fired up. I thought that I had better take a poke of gold dust down to the bank in Dawson. I had a large poke which held about $8,000 at $16 an ounce. It weighed a lot as gold is quite heavy. I went to Grand Forks as I knew there would be some freighters going to Dawson and I could get a ride. A man was just getting a team of horses out of a stable, and seeing the sleigh near with a flat top, which I thought was his, I threw my sack of gold dust on it. I had put the poke in a gunny sack. I went and asked the man if he was going to Dawson. He said he was and for me to come along.

I helped him hitch up the team and we went down to Dawson. He asked me where I was going and I told him the Canadian Bank of Commerce. "Oh," he said, "I go right by there."

When he saw me getting my sack off the sleigh and saw the way I had to lift it, he knew at once it was a lot of gold dust. Then he said, "You damn fool, you just threw that sack on the sleigh and never once turned to look at it all the way here. You must be loony but you look all right."

We finally got the dump all sluiced up and we had quite a lot of gold dust at $16 an ounce—$127,000.

CHEECHAKO

Chapter eleven

Nome

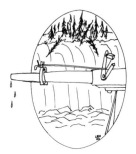

What to do now? For some time we had been hearing about a gold strike away down at a place called Nome and we thought perhaps we might go there.

One day, while we were deciding what to do, I went down Bonanza Creek to Trail Creek. It was only about six or eight miles from Dawson. On that creek about a half mile up, four men were mining a hillside claim in the same White Channel that ran through Gold Hill and others. This claim was low grade. I panned around and could only get about ten cents to the pan, but the paystreak was about four feet or more.

Somehow I wanted a claim before going to Nome, if we went. I offered these men $4,000. They wanted $5,000 but they took the $4,000. They wanted to go to Nome too.

Several times when in Dawson I went to see that doctor to get the $200 I had loaned him, but he always had a lot of reasons why he could not pay me just then.

We turned our Gold Hill claim over to a man who thought he might be able to work it and get out a little money, but he was unable to do so. A few years later a large mining company mined all the hillsides and creeks and hydraulicked everything. Doing it that way they made a lot of money.

About the 20th of June, there was a river steamer, the "Hamilton," leaving Dawson for St. Michael, so Jim and I took passage on it. We would take an ocean boat over to Nome. The "Hamilton" had a full load of passengers, all bound for Nome, the new gold find. We got down to the mouth of the Yukon all right and found that the Bering Sea was still frozen over and nothing to do but wait. Soon more river boats came along all loaded with passengers going to Nome. The pastime for most of the passengers was gambling, but Jim and I had never gambled and did not then.

On the 30th of June we were able to leave the mouth of the Yukon and go into the Bering Sea, staying pretty close along shore to the head of a canal. This canal runs sixteen miles winding around and into the St. Michael Bay. There was no ice in the Canal, but the Bay was not open. The other way around to St. Michael, through Stephens Pass, was still frozen over.

Soon all the river boats were tied up in the head of the canal. There a small steamer from the Holy Cross Mission came alongside. They had been at the south mouth of the Yukon and had caught a lot of the first run of king salmon, some weighing fifty pounds and more. The river boats were all getting short of provisions and when our steward saw those fish he immediately bought them all. I think that the king salmon at the south mouth of the Yukon are the best salmon in the world.

It was the morning of the third of July, 1900, when we got to St. Michael, which is very late. Generally you can get to St. Michael about the middle of June.

After more waiting we did get aboard a ship going across the Bering Sea to Nome. The ocean boats from Seattle and elsewhere discharged their cargoes at St. Michael. The river boats get their loads here for along the Yukon, and Dawson, 1600 miles up the Yukon.

Arriving at Nome, we could find no hotel accommodations. We bought a tent and set it up on the beach. There were lots of men rocking on the beach and some got quite a little gold. We stayed in Nome three or four days. One day I walked out to Anvil Creek, one of the richest creeks, and not very far—I think only about eight miles from Nome.

Jim and I decided to go on to Seattle. So we went to the steamship office and bought our tickets. Soon a ship came and anchored off shore. However, it was found that they had smallpox aboard and no one was allowed to come ashore or go aboard, I guess, for a couple of weeks or more.

We did not know what to do, so went back out to Anvil Creek and over to Dexter Creek also. Between those two creeks they had started looking for gold and the first thing I knew Jim had bought a claim from a miner who was only down a few feet with his shaft. Jim bought his tent and camping outfit, then we went into Nome to get more supplies.

That night we heard of a new strike and, of course, it was much better than any other strike! Anyway, I told Jim to hire a man or two to help him sink the shaft and I went on this new stampede. I should have known better, but that is the way it is when you hear of a new gold strike.

We had already gone back to the steamship ticket office and they had refunded our ticket money.

CHEECHAKO

Chapter Twelve

Lavelle Young

Arriving back in Nome after that wild and useless stampede, I met two men from Dawson that I knew, Tom Bruce and George Crummy. After talking for some time, Tom said that before freeze-up there would be a lot of travel back to Dawson on the Yukon River. He knew of a river boat that could be bought and which would more than pay for itself on one trip with a load of passengers and freight.

This boat, the steamer "Lavelle Young," was anchored in St. Michael harbor and could be bought for $20,000. Bruce had only $1,500 and Crummy had $800, and I would have to put up the rest. Anyone with the least bit of common sense would have had nothing to do with that kind of a deal, especially when we knew absolutely nothing about steamboating!

But fool that I was, I agreed; and we bought the boat from an agent in Nome, paying only half down.

Time seems to go fast! It was now the middle of August and we figured we should leave St. Michael for Dawson September 1, and put an ad in a Nome newspaper to that effect.

At the claim between the heads of Anvil and Dexter Creeks, Jim didn't do so well. He had never mined any only in the Dawson country where any Cheechako would know when he reached bedrock and in placer mining the gold is on and just above bedrock. After going down over a hundred feet, Jim found nothing and quit. Someone else who

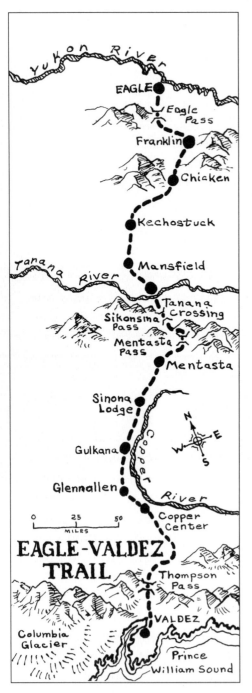

EAGLE-VALDEZ TRAIL

knew what the bedrock was like here, went down to the eighty-foot level, drifted in a short distance and struck it real good. Jim had gone out to Seattle before this happened—he was smart enough to want nothing to do with a steamboat.

Bruce, Crummy and I went over to St. Michael and found our steamer anchored in the harbor. Captain Betts was aboard as watchman and he also represented the owners who were in Portland, Oregon. We got busy, hired a Captain and pilot, first and second engineers, first mate (Crummy was going to act as second mate). We also had to get firemen and deck hands. Bruce was to be the steward. He was a restaurant man from Dawson. I became the purser. We had brought a lot of supplies over from Nome and could also get most anything in St. Michael.

We did not know anything about the men we were hiring, especially the officers. The Captain we engaged proceeded to bring aboard a five-gallon jug of whiskey and got drunk so we let him go.

In a few days we had our passengers come over from Nome about a hundred of them. We had also taken on a hundred tons of freight from one of the companies.

At that time the passenger fare to Dawson was $125 and freight was $100 per ton. Finally we got started. We went around through Stephens Pass and on to the mouth of the Yukon which is seventy miles from St. Michael and can be made only in good weather by a river boat. We tied up about forty miles up the river to wash the boiler.

After entering the fresh river water from the salty Bering Sea you have to cool down and wash the salt out of the boiler. The boiler must be cooled down very slowly. After washing, the boiler must be heated to get steam up again very slowly. It lasted about twenty hours.

There was a large drift pile close by. The crew cut quite a lot of wood for our boiler. I helped and so did some of the passengers, those who could tear themselves away from gambling, which was going on all the time.

One hundred and twenty-eight miles up the Yukon, the Andreafsky River comes into the Yukon. We had reached few miles below there, when the engineer said there was a leak in the boiler. We tied up and found there was a crack in the flue sheet caused by getting steam up too fast after washing it. The engineers said the boiler was useless and we could go no further.

Talk about calamity—this was it! The next day the steamer "Sarah" came along and we signaled her to stop. She came alongside and I made arrangements for her to take all our passengers and freight to Dawson so everything was transferred aboard the "Sarah."

Those bum, drunken engineers of ours said they could keep up enough steam on our leaky boiler to get back to St. Michael. A new boiler could be brought up from Seattle next spring and installed. Bruce and Crummy went back with the boat to St. Michael and put her in winter quarters. Crummy stayed on as watchman and Bruce went to Seattle.

I had to go on to Dawson on the steamer "Hannah" to get quite a lot of gold dust up there which I wanted to take out to Seattle.

It was a long, uneventful trip up the river to Dawson except that I became acquainted with a nice young girl, Sarah Elliot. She and her father were passengers. He was going up to look after some mining interests. He had a couple of claims near Dawson and his daughter was going to keep house for him.

Sarah and I got to like each other a great deal and now I thought I was really in love! I asked Sarah to marry me, and was accepted. Her father did not like the business I was in—owning a steamboat was much too risky! He would not hear of us getting married now and just to wait—said we had plenty of time.

It was getting late in the season now and the last boat was soon to leave Dawson for Whitehorse so I had to go, telling Sarah I would be back next summer.

Arriving in Whitehorse, I took the White Pass train to Skagway then a boat to Seattle. There I disposed of my gold dust and met Captain Betts, to pay the balance I owed on the "Lavelle Young." We still owed $10,000. Captain Betts was very fair. He said he knew we had had very bad luck with the steamer and he would accept $5,000 in full payment.

I was more than pleased. A person could not have had much worse luck than had happened to us. We still had to buy a new boiler and get it to St. Michael and installed!

CHEECHAKO

Chapter thirteen

Home

In a few days I left Seattle and went home to the farm in Bruce, North Dakota. My mother and younger brother, Howard, were the only ones on the farm now. They were glad to see me. They soon wanted to know from whom I was getting all those letters, and I told them about Sarah.

My mother and brother Howard, two years younger than I, were getting tired of the farm. I told them to sell it and come to Seattle where Mother could live and Howard could go with me to Dawson. This they did, selling the farm and then held an auction, selling the stock, horses, cows and everything else. In February we went to Seattle and rented a house for Mother and a sister, Mary, who had quit her job in St. Paul, Minnesota, and came out with us.

In the meantime I had gone to see my brother George. He agreed to come out to Seattle later on, buy a steamboat boiler, and come with it up to St. Michael where I would meet him. My brother Howard and I planned to buy twenty tons of goods, perishables and other things, and take them into Dawson to sell as Herman Mueller and I had done.

This time we bought everything in Seattle, including a horse, and had it all shipped to Whitehorse. The White Pass Railroad was now operating between Skagway and Whitehorse. We arrived in Whitehorse in April, set up a large tent with a stove in it to keep the perishables from freezing, and one of us had to stay and keep a fire in the stove all the time until the weather got warm.

We made camp at the foot of Lake Laberge and brought everything down there but the perishables. We hired a freighter to move them to the lake and from there we could do it ourselves. We found out, though, that we needed another man, so hired a man, and everything went along all right.

We got the lumber for the scow down to the foot of the lake and I stayed there to build the scow. By the time the Yukon was open to Dawson we were on our way. We had to wait at only one place for an ice jam to clear out. We got a good price for everything in Dawson. Howard was very pleased.

We were going to St. Michael to see about getting the "Lavelle" ready but no boats were leaving for downriver until they figured the Bering Sea would be open. Howard and I went up to Trail Creek to my claim and we worked there for two weeks or more extending the tunnel. Finally we went to Dawson and got aboard the first boat to leave for St. Michael.

We had to wait a few days at the mouth for the ice to clear out of the Sea. One day, while waiting, I went on the tundra to see if I could get a jack rabbit. I had a 22 rifle. I saw something sitting up which I thought much too large for a rabbit but shot it anyway. It was a jack rabbit and in dragging it by the hind foot back to the boat, most of it was on the ground. The steward told me that three or four like that would feed everyone on the ship.

My brother George had bought a steamboat boiler in Seattle. He chartered a sailing vessel, loaded it with coal and the boiler, and sailed for St. Michael, arriving there a few days after we did. We had the "Lavelle Young" towed alongside the ship and the boiler was put aboard. The ship then went to Nome and Golovin with Howard aboard and he sold all the coal. There is no timber around Nome or any place around the Bering Sea.

George figured that the boiler did not cost them anything.

We soon had the "Young" ready and got a load of 300 tons of general merchandise to take to Dawson. Tom Bruce had arrived from Seattle and soon we were on our way. Howard went to Seattle to get Mother and take her into Dawson and up to the claim. Mother did not like to stay alone in Seattle. She wanted to be with Howard and me.

We made the trip to Dawson though and wintered the "Young" in a slough just above Dawson. I went to work with Howard on the claim. George went out home.

Howard and I got the tunnel driven to the back of the mine so we could crosscut and then work forward. This ground was not frozen. It was very dry. The front of the tunnel had to be lowered and some of it was solid rock. We had to use dynamite to blast it out. The dynamite was frozen and had to be thawed out.

I was thawing a few sticks on the top of the cabin stove one day. I just rolled them around on top of the stove; had four sticks that time, holding three of them in one hand while I was rolling the last one around on the stove. A drop of glycerin dropped on the stove and went off like a rifle shot.

That was all that happened, but it scared me almost to death. I got an awful calling down from Howard when he heard what I had done. Said he did not care about me, but did not want our mother blown to bits. After that, we rigged up a place in a side tunnel in the mine and thawed the dynamite out there.

We got the tunnel down enough so it was level all the way out from the back, laid a good iron rail track, had two cars made and hired two men. Where we started cross-cutting the back of the claim we found better pay there than out near the front.

Mother liked it very much at the mine. She became acquainted with two other ladies whose husbands were working a claim nearby. One day a big yellow tom cat came around. He was hungry, and we fed him and he just stayed on. We made a yarn ball one evening after supper and would throw it around the cabin for the cat to chase. We taught him to bring it to us and we would throw it again.

After a few days, the cat would come and jump up in our laps after supper and we would have to throw the ball for him to chase. We started hiding the ball and he would keep looking around until he found it. One day we put the ball inside a pair of leather shoes. It took him a day to find it, but he did.

One evening we hid the ball a way down inside one of our pillow cases. That poor cat looked for three days until he found it, and was he not pleased with himself!

Mr. Cat wanted to follow us into the mine and we would chase him out. We were afraid he would get run over by the ore cars. The tunnel was dark and the ore cars heavy when loaded. Well, poor Mr. Cat was run over and killed one day. We were all so sorry but what could we do.

We kept on working that spring until it was time to make sluice boxes and get them set up to wash out our dump. Trail Gulch had enough water in the early spring to wash up all the dumps, and we got a nice sum of money out of ours. I sure made no mistake when I bought this claim.

I gave Howard a half interest in the claim and he kept on working while I went to get the "Young" ready to go to St. Michael. The Bering Sea doesn't open until about the middle of June so we had lots of time. Tom Bruce had a restaurant in Dawson at this time but he came along with us. Before leaving Dawson, I made arrangements with J. E. Lilly & Company to bring up for them 300 tons of merchandise which he would ship to St. Michael from Seattle later.

During that winter I went twice to see Sarah. Her father was mining on Dominion Creek quite a distance from Trail Gulch. Her father was very pleased to hear that I was now mining. He said, "If only you would give up that crazy steamboating!" I told him I might later on, so Sarah and I thought it best to wait for a while before getting married.

CHEECHAKO

Chapter fourteen

Captain Barnette

We took the "Lavelle Young" down to St. Michael arriving there about the middle of June. Captain Barnette was there waiting for a shipment of trading goods to arrive from Seattle. He had a small stern wheel steamer with which he intended to take a large stock of goods up the Tanana River and start a trading post.

In July, 1901, while moving around the Bay he struck a rock with this steamer and it sunk. I think it was called the "Arctic Bay"; anyway he was unable to do anything with it.

Captain Barnette came over to see me about taking his supplies up the Tanana River to Tanana Crossing. None of us had ever been up the Tanana River, but I heard that Captain Patterson had been up there with a small launch bringing log rafts down for the United States Army at Fort Weare, which is now called Tanana. Captain Patterson was in St. Michael at that time and I went to see him. He told me that the "Lavelle Young" could not go up the Tanana farther than the mouth of Chena Slough. He also gave me the names of two pilots that I could get at Fort Weare.

I then told Captain Barnette that it was very doubtful if we could get beyond Chena Slough. After some talk we made up a contract whereby we agreed to take him to the Slough for so much a ton and if possible, to take him and his outfit of 130 tons to Tanana Crossing for an additional sum per ton.

It was also agreed that if we got beyond Chena Slough and could get no farther, that Barnette would get off with his goods wherever that happened to be.

So we took his goods aboard, and also Mrs. Barnett, Mr. Smith (who was some kind of a partner) and three men. In the outfit he also had a dog team and a horse.

We left St. Michael about the 8th of August and had no trouble reaching Fort Weare near the mouth of the Tanana. There we got the two pilots. In going up the Tanana we had to cut our own wood for the boiler, stopping each evening when we saw some dry trees.

We finally passed the mouth of Chena Slough, and a mile or so above, Hendericks & Belt had a trading post. We went on up six or eight miles and came to where the river was all scattered out in a lot of channels, none of which was deep enough for us. The "Lavelle Young" was not a light draft steamer and we did not have steam steering gear or a steam capstan.

After trying all the channels, our Captain (I think his name was Fredericks) told me it was impossible to go farther and Captain Barnette agreed with him.

Captain Barnette then told me that an Indian had told him that perhaps we could go up the Chena Slough and get out into the Tanana again above this bad place and go on up to the Crossing. This we decided to do. We went back and started up the slough. We reached a point about six miles above where Fairbanks now is. Here we could get no farther. This was just before noon and we tied up.

I then told Captain Barnette that according to the contract he should get off here, but he wanted me to take him down to the mouth of the slough.

Going downstream is much more difficult than going up. I figured we would perhaps get stuck a few times. So would not agree to take him that far unless he would pay us for the time lost while stuck. He also figured we would get stuck on a bar, perhaps more than once, and refused.

We were in the pilot house alone, and after an hour or so of debate he said that he had noticed a nice high, heavily wooded bank about six miles below and asked me to take him there. I agreed to do so. On the way down we got stuck twice, but not bad, and finally tied up right where the Northern Commercial Co. store now stands in the town of Fairbanks. This was August 26, 1901, about four o'clock.

At 5 P.M. Angus McDougall, a deck-hand, cut the first tree down which was leaning over the bank and close to the pilot house; the second tree was cut by Shorty Robinson; and the third by Soapy Smith II. We had to clear a space in the timber to pile Barnett's goods ashore and also so he could erect some large tents.

The second day while unloading, two prospectors came along. They said they were prospecting on a creek which later turned out to be Gold Stream or a branch of it. They bought some bacon and things from Barnette and also showed us some gold dust—just a little from where they were prospecting; then they went back. One of those men was Felix Pedro.

The next morning our Japanese cook, after drinking a lot of something besides water, fell overboard. He was a good swimmer and got out all right.

It looked very bad for Captain Barnette to be put off there with no Indians or anyone else to trade with. Just before we left one of our deck-hands, Dan McCarty, came to me and said he would like to stay and that one of Barnette's men would take his place. So I paid Dan and took the other man. Dan later found a good claim—he and his father, I believe.

Mrs. Barnette was crying when we left the next day, as it did not look good to her either.

Captain Barnette was quite angry with me because I would not take him to the mouth of the slough, but late that winter I saw him in Dawson on his way outside and he was all smiles. He told me that I could not have put him off in a better place!

CHEECHAKO

Chapter fifteen

Mother

We got back to St. Michael after taking Barnette up the Tanana River and soon the ocean boat arrived from Seattle with J. E. Lilly's freight—300 tons—all hay and oats. We stowed the oats in the hold of the "Young" and the hay on deck. We made it up to Dawson and after tying the boat up in the slough for the winter, I went up to Trail Gulch to work in the mine.

After a few days, I went out to see Sarah. Her father had worked his claim out and they had gone outside so that ended another love affair of mine.

I worked in the mine all winter with Howard. In the spring we got the "Lavelle Young" ready to go down the river. Now the big stampede was on to the Fairbanks country where I had left Barnette—he had named it Fairbanks. We got a load of passengers and freight for Fairbanks and started down the river, but first I contracted with Lilly & Company to bring up their freight from St. Michael.

My mother wanted to take a trip so she came along; she liked traveling on boats, especially on ships at sea. We made it to Fairbanks all right and then on to St. Michael, got our load of freight and back to Dawson. We did not have a barge and the "Young" drew quite a lot of water when loaded. We got stuck once on the way up but only for a few hours. We discharged our cargo in Dawson and back for another load.

This time on the way upriver, about 30 miles above Fort Weare (now called Tanana), the captain, Captain Blair, ran against a rock and punched a hole in our bow. A lot of water came in before we got it stopped and could back off, and a great many sacks of oats got wet. We had these wet sacks taken up on the hurricane deck where the oats were spread out on deck. The oats soon dried and were resacked. While drying, a lot of cinders from the smokestack got into them. That winter Miss Lilly of the firm of Lilly and Co. asked me how cinders got into the oats—and I did not seem to know. Anyway, wood cinders are not injurious to horses.

We went back to St. Michael for our last load that season. Now the river had fallen very low and at Coal Creek above Circle City, we could not make the crossing. We had to cache some hay and oats in order to get across—then on to Dawson.

Before the river closed, Howard and Mother went outside. They were going to make a home in Whittier, California. From Seattle, they took an ocean boat for Los Angeles because Mother liked to travel on the ocean. About a day out from Seattle, the ship, "The Queen," caught fire. They put all the women and children off in life boats, thinking they might not be able to put out the fire. The boat Mother was in capsized and all in it were thrown into the water. They put out the fire and got everyone aboard again. But Mother died from the shock. Howard wired me about it, then came back to Dawson.

I was working in the mine when that wire came. It was phoned up to a roadhouse at the foot of Trail Gulch about a quarter of a mile from my claim. The lady who owned the roadhouse sent a man up to tell me to come down. She told me in the nicest possible way that she had a telegram for me and that it was bad news. Then she read the telegram and it was bad news—the worst possible news—and it took me a long time to get over it. Mother was always so good and wonderful to us. She was the best mother in the world.

In November, I think it was, Tom Bruce wrote and asked me to come to Dawson. He said that the Agent of the Alaska Commercial Co. wanted to see us. I went down one day and Bruce, Crummy and I went to see this Agent. The Alaska Commercial Co. had a lot of steamboats on the river and they did not want independent boats around. He wanted to buy our steamer "Lavelle Young." After some dickering, we settled for $15,000. This money was all mine and Bruce and Crummy still owed me quite a lot.

Later on I settled up with Bruce by knocking a lot off but Crummy never did pay up.

Now it was back to the mine. I was lucky to have bought it.

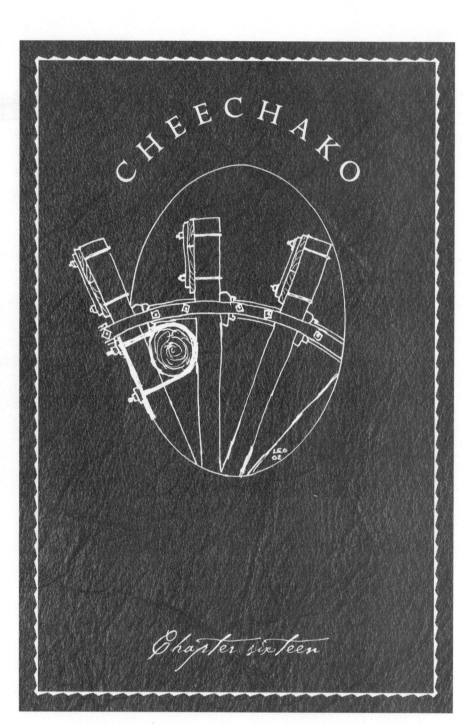

CHEECHAKO

Chapter sixteen

Oil City

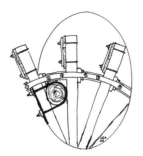

The next spring—April, 1900—the Agent of the Standard Oil Co sent for me. He wanted to sell me a steamboat. The Oil Company had a large steamboat and it was laid up in the Andreafsky River which enters the Yukon 128 miles from St. Michael. The name of this boat was "Oil City." She was 175 feet long; the "Lavelle Young" was only 150 feet long.

Why I ever considered buying another steamboat I will never know. I had a little money now and a claim where I could dig up some more. Why should I have been so foolish as to buy another boat?—but I did. I gave them $7,500 for it.

When I told Howard, he said, "Well, I always thought you were crazy and now I know you are."

After buying the "Oil City," I engaged a man named Anderson to go out to Seattle and have a large barge built for the "Oil City" to tow; a barge that would carry 400 tons of freight. I contracted with J. E. Lilly & Co. to bring up all their freight from St. Michael which consisted mostly of hay and oats.

When it was time for the first steamer to go down river, I hired two engineers, a fireman, a mate, a cook and a waiter. The first boat went down as far as Tanana then it went up the Tanana River to Fairbanks, and then back to Dawson. We got off at Tanana. There I bought two small row boats, hired a couple of deck hands and we floated and rowed down to Andreafsky and boarded the "Oil City." We started to get her ready to go to St. Michael.

After about three weeks, the first boat going to St. Michael came along. On it was a Captain Moore and a pilot that I had engaged before leaving Dawson so we started for St. Michael. Here I hired a full crew.

Lilly's freight came in but my barge did not, being delayed somehow. We took all we could aboard the "Oil City" and I got the Alaska Commercial Co. to take the balance. We made it to Dawson all right. My brother George had come aboard at St. Michael. He had staked me to start with and had a half interest in everything. In Dawson he came to me and said he did not like steamboating. I gave him my half interest in the mine and I took the steamboat. I had already given Howard a half interest in the mine.

I got a load of freight and a lot of passengers for Fairbanks and down the river we started. We got along all right until we were below Fort Yukon where the pilot ran into a wrong channel. We were stuck bad but did manage in a day or so to get off and on down to Tanana. There we left the Yukon and started up the Tanana River for Fairbanks.

Sixty miles up the Tanana while going along, we felt a tremendous jar which shook the whole boat. They got the boat tied up alongside a wooded bank and found that our wheel shaft was broken. Ours was a split wheel and it broke right in the middle. This was a terrible accident.

Our chief engineer, John Trout, said we could try putting four logs across the wheel and take down some of our iron hog chains to make stirrups. We got four good logs by cutting down four good trees and stirruped that wheel together. While working at the wheel, the steamer "Cudahy" came along on the way to Fairbanks and she took all our passengers which cost me quite a lot.

While they were working on the wheel, a custom house man and I took a small boat and went down river a few miles to a telegraph station. I wanted to find out if I could get a shaft at St. Michael from some of the company's old boats there and found that I could not.

And then another blow—a wire came for me from Anderson whom I had sent out from Dawson to Ballard to have a barge built. This wire said that while being towed across the Gulf of Alaska, they got into a bad storm and lost the barge. This was indeed a terrible blow. Seemed I was having nothing but trouble.

We got back to the "Oil City" and in another day or so we had the wheel fixed so started up the river again. By going along carefully and not trying to run a race with anyone, we made it up to Chena, about ten miles below Fairbanks. We put the freight off here. This was as far as I had agreed to take it. There were a number of little boats running up from here.

I want to say here that without our second engineer we could never have made all those stirrups that held our wheel together.

Soon we were on our way downriver to St. Michael. In a few days our freight came in from Seattle and having no barge, there was 400 tons that I had to give to the other companies to take to Dawson.

The "Oil City" would carry only about 100 tons. Leaving St. Michael, we made it up to a place twelve miles above Fort Yukon where it was so shallow that it was impossible for us to make it. On a good bank we cached 100 tons of hay. This lightened us up enough so we could make it.

In these swift and shallow places we had difficulty in starting. We had a good ship's carpenter aboard and he made two monkey rudders, rigged them up with wooden stocks and on we went to Dawson. After discharging the freight, we put the "Oil City" in winter quarters in the slough above Dawson.

Who should I meet one day but Sarah. Such a pleasant surprise! Her father had bought an interest in a mining claim and she was working in a ladies' furnishings store. Now I did not have to walk thirty or forty miles to see her.

CHEECHAKO

Chapter seventeen

New Partners

One day Bert Dickey of the Dominion Commercial Co. and Billy Clark of Mersereaud & Clark came to see me and wanted to know if I would sell a half interest in the "Oil City." The "Oil City" had a broken shaft and a broken owner and it did not take long to come to terms. I sold them a half interest for $6,000.

There were three men in the Dominion Commercial Co. Mr. Daub, who scowed the goods down from Whitehorse, a Mr. Schockenback who recovered the goods in Dawson and had freighters take them out to the creeks where Dickey sold them to the miners. The firm of Mersereaud & Clark had just two partners, Andy Mersereaud who ran the goods down from Whitehorse and Clark who sold them in Dawson.

We had to get a new shaft for the "Oil City" and sent out to the East Coast for a hollow steel shaft. It was said that a hollow shaft would not break as a solid shaft does once in a while. This shaft was to be shipped to Seattle. Then we could have it shipped to Whitehorse. From there it was up to us to get it to Dawson. I think it weighed six or eight tons.

Daub took charge of getting the shaft from Whitehorse to the foot of the lake. He had lumber sent in with which to build a scow and hired a freighter to take the shaft and lumber down. He then built a scow, got the shaft aboard and when the river opened, came on to Dawson.

I stayed aboard the "Oil City" all winter. In the spring I had a crew come in from Seattle; Captain De Pue and John Trout who was Chief Engineer came with them. A few days before the shaft arrived we had the "Oil City" ready and moved over to Dawson where we installed the shaft and built a new wheel.

Before leaving the slough, we were able to buy a small river boat. Her machinery had been taken out and we used her as a barge. She would carry about 100 tons. Mersereaud & Clark and the Dominion Commercial Co. were leaving Dawson and going to Fairbanks, so when the "Oil City" was ready they came aboard. There was Mr. and Mrs. Dicky and Clark, and a lot of freight. We had to leave room for the 100 tons I had cached above Fort Yukon.

We got along all right until about twenty miles below Circle where Captain De Pue took a wrong channel and we were stuck quite bad. It took a day to get off. I was acting as purser but had been in the pilot house a lot and knew the river well. Someone told the Captain that I knew the river better than anyone. He sent for me, told me what he had heard and asked me to show him the right channels which I did and we had no more getting stuck.

We picked up that 100 tons of hay that I had cached and on to Chena about ten miles below Fairbanks. The "Oil City" was too heavy to go up the slough to Fairbanks. Soon as the freight was discharged, we started down river for St. Michael.

Captain De Pue had an electric bell rigged up from the pilot house to the purser's office and when he would get lost, he would ring for me and I would go up and tell him where the right channel was.

Mr. Daub was with us but before leaving Seattle he had bought lumber to build a large barge and had it shipped to St. Michael. He had engaged a contractor to come along with a crew of men and build the barge in St. Michael. The contractor, Tom Trahey, arrived in St. Michael soon after we did, with the barge material and crew of carpenters.

Captain De Pue said he knew how the barge should be built so it would not draw much water which would be a big advantage in going up a shallow river like the Tanana. Trahey was to build it according to De Pue's blueprint.

Our freight came along from Seattle. When the "Oil City" and small barge were loaded, Daub thought that I should stay in St. Michael and see that they got along all right building the barge. I did although it was not necessary.

Trahey did not like the way the barge was to be built because it had no solid keelsons—just props to hold up the deck. But the barge was built and launched before the "Oil City" got back.

The "Oil City" had a lot of trouble on the Tanana River going up—got stuck on a bar and in some way sank the barge about twenty miles below Chena. They had to go to Chena, unload the "Oil City," then back to the barge, and get what freight they could and take it up. They found that the barge was too badly damaged to be of any use so left it there, more than half sunk.

Our new barge was called the "Irene." The ship with our freight came in to anchor in the harbor and we went alongside with the "Oil City" and "Irene" and started to load. Nothing is put in the hold of these river barges—everything stowed on deck—and they have good houses on them.

I was out on the bow of the "Irene" checking freight and she was about two-thirds loaded when there was a great crash of some kind. The whole barge shook. The deck hands who were stowing freight, came running out and the barge slowly sank. We all had time to get aboard the ship.

Without any solid keelsons to hold the deck up, it caved in when there was about 100 tons on it. There was our new barge with just about a foot of the roof out of the water. We were able to tow it into the harbor to a sloping beach. When each tide would come in, we got it up a little, took off some freight and each day we got it a little higher. This way we had the barge all unloaded and out of the water.

Leaving Seattle, the freight was all insured so was not a total loss.

Daub took all the canned goods over to Nome and sold them. While there, he was able to get material to build keelsons in the "Irene" and started to work.

The Cold Storage Company had a barge which we were able to rent.

We got all our freight that was left on to the barge and with the "Oil City" made the trip to Chena and back without trouble. Since the "Irene" was all fixed up, we had two barges for the last trip of the season and no more trouble.

We tied up for the winter in front of Chena. Next spring, 1906, when the ice broke and commenced to run, I heard a commotion early one morning. Looking up ahead a short distance, I saw the steamer "Rock Island" leaning over badly, then she sank. A big piece of ice had struck her hull and punched a big hole in it. Several boats and barges were tied up right in the river channel.

Our crew for the "Oil City" came in from Seattle and we got ready to head for St. Michael. As soon as the ice cleared we started down river, reaching St. Michael about the middle of June. Our freight soon came in from Seattle and we got our two barges loaded and made it up to Chena and Fairbanks. Then we made another trip in good shape.

But on the third trip up from St. Michael, on arriving at the mouth of the Tanana River we found the water so low that we could not get through the mouth with our heavily loaded barges, and the "Oil City" was also heavy.

We tried several different channels but there was not enough water. Now what to do? It looked very bad for us.

Captain Langley, with his steamer "Wilbur Crimmins," and a small barge, was tied up at the town of Tanana near the mouth of the Tanana River. We bought his boat and barge. His steamer was small and light draft so with her help and a bit of trouble, we finally got to Chena. That little steamer was a Godsend to us. Without her we could never have made it. We took the two boats and barge down to a slough four miles below Chena, tying them there for the winter.

Mr. Daub and I had decided that we needed two more barges—a small one for the steamer "Crimmins" and a larger one for the "Oil City." We would build them at the foot of Lake Laberge the following spring. After staying around Fairbanks for about a month, he went out to Seattle by way of Valdez.

CHEECHAKO

LEO
02

Chapter eighteen

Sarah

I wanted to see Sarah so I teamed up with Henry Isaacks, a clothing merchant of the firm of Isaacks Bros. He wanted to go outside by way of Dawson.

We bought a small horse and a sleigh and started about the first of November. We got some hay and oats for the horse and very little in the grub line for ourselves as we would find roadhouses all along the trail. We did take a couple of blankets and Henry had a gallon jug of whiskey.

Leaving Fairbanks one morning, we made Chatanika that evening on a good trail made by the freighters hauling supplies to the miners. On our second day we had to go up the Chatanika River about forty miles to a roadhouse. This little river was, of course, frozen over. That day it had started to snow a heavy wet snow. Soon we found it hard going. We knew we could never make the roadhouse that night.

Late in the afternoon we saw a deserted miner's cabin where we gladly stopped for the night. We had a good warm blanket for the horse and hay and oats for him to eat. I made a campfire and cooked some bacon and canned beans. I also made tea and we had the usual hardtack.

Henry was not accustomed to walking or roughing it. He sat in the sleigh all day while I walked most of the time ahead of the horse. I was wearing moccasins and could feel where the trail was under the snow. Left alone, the horse kept getting off the trail.

That night Henry had a little drink of whiskey. He never took too much and he could not understand why I would not have any. Water or tea was all I wanted. I had never tasted liquor. I had tasted beer once and did not like it.

Next morning it was still snowing but we started out and just at dark made the roadhouse. You don't know how good that roadhouse looked to us and what a meal we had—moose steaks and everything! A party of moose hunters came along soon after we did. They had quite a large dog team. They planned to get a moose or two and take them down to Fairbanks to sell to the restaurants. Tom Gibson was one of the men. They were going up to the head of Twelve Mile Creek and we had to go that way also.

It had quit snowing and we all got started. A horse can travel much better than dogs in heavy snow so I went ahead, the horse following and then the dogs. We hoped to make it to the Summit roadhouse just over Twelve Mile Summit but the going was too hard and we all had to camp this side of the Summit, all tired and worn out.

The hunters were going to hunt in this neighborhood but we had to go on. Knowing that the snow would be much deeper on Twelve Mile Summit, we got them to help us over to the roadhouse. At one place we had to shovel our way through the snow for our horse and sleigh.

After a hard day, we did make it over and down to the roadhouse which was run by two men. One had gone after supplies with his dog team and had not yet got back. All there was to eat was caribou stew, sourdough bread and tea.

Next morning we paid the hunters for helping us and they left. They did not want to take any pay. Henry and I stayed there two more days because the trail was unbroken. All this time we had nothing to eat but caribou stew three times a day. Our horse got along better than we did.

We left the second morning and made it to an empty cabin, a distance of 14 miles of hard going through the snow. On getting out our grub box we found we had only four hardtack and tea.

Henry said, "What are we going to do? It is a long way to the next roadhouse at the foot of Eagle Pass and much as I dislike caribou meat, right now I wish we had some."

Before we left the caribou roadhouse, I knew we had eaten up all our grub from the hunters so I had gotten four caribou steaks from our host without letting Henry know. I brought them out and cooked two that evening and two the next morning.

Just as we were getting started, a man came along with a big team of horses and a sleigh from a mining camp below so we followed him all day with nothing to eat. He had nothing either and was on his way to get supplies. That was a long, hard day. I walked all the time which was not so bad except I became very hungry.

Just after dark, we made it to the Eagle roadhouse. They had lots of grub and a good cook and we ate like starving men. After a good breakfast next morning, we started over the pass. I think it is 4000 feet high. We got to the top all right and found the going much better on the other side so we had no trouble making the next roadhouse by nightfall. This was a very fine roadhouse and they also had a good cook.

They told us that we were a little too early to travel on the Yukon River. The ice was not solid yet. It is only sixty miles from here to Circle City which is on the Yukon. We decided to go over to the Circle Hot Springs, twenty miles or so and stay a few days. Circle Hot Springs is quite famous—lots of people go there, and we found wonderful hot water bubbling out of the ground. The baths were so good—and we needed a bath after all those days.

We stayed four days; then on again to Circle City where we stayed two days. There we met Andy Mersereaud of the Mersereaud & Clark firm in Fairbanks, who had an interest in the "Oil City." They had sold goods to the miners back of Circle and Andy was collecting for them and had been paid in gold dust. He wanted to go to Dawson and on out to Seattle so came along with us.

The morning we left Circle, it had turned cold and was 50° below. The first roadhouse up the Yukon was about thirty miles, which we made without any trouble. The next day we had to make only about twenty-five miles. There was a strong downstream wind blowing with the temperature 35° below zero; and we had a hard time to keep from getting frost-bitten.

We each had on fur coats but the wind would blow right through them. We also wore fur gauntlet mittens which we could hold against our faces but, even so, our cheeks and chins were frost-bitten. We made the roadhouse Woodchopper and such a relief to get inside, away from that terrible wind!

The wind quit during the night so next morning we were on our way and made Coal Creek that evening.

The following afternoon we were going along minding our own business when, all at once, the horse broke through the ice and into the river with just his head above water. The sleigh did not break through. I grabbed the horse's bridle and held well up while Andy unhitched him from the sleigh, pulling it back out of the way. Then Andy went ashore with the axe, got a good, stout little tree and trimmed the branches off making a strong pole about fifteen feet long. He put it under the horse just back of his front legs. Then he and Henry pried down lifting the horse up. I was also pulling and the horse got his front legs out onto solid ice. Then they put the pole just forward of his hind legs and prying down got the horse all the way out. By this time the poor little horse was very cold and did not want to move after he was hitched up. We had to switch him with a stout willow to get him going. He soon got warmed up and was all right.

Andy Mersereaud deserves all the credit for getting the horse out of the river. I did not know how to do it. Henry, I guess, knew a lot about men's clothing but nothing about a horse.

It was lucky that the sleigh stayed up with that $60,000 in gold dust on it—gold dust is very heavy!

It became dark long before we could reach a roadhouse and, as we did not like to travel after dark on the river, we stopped when we saw a cabin. We found it deserted and stayed there all night. We had plenty of feed for the horse and we had bacon, canned beans and a loaf of bread.

The next day we made Nation. Then on up to Eagle which is fifty miles below Forty Mile and from there to Dawson, another fifty-two miles. Dawson is about 400 miles from Fairbanks.

We made Dawson all right and sold the horse. Henry and Andy went on outside on the White Pass Railroad which ran a stage overland from Dawson to Whitehorse and then the railroad from Whitehorse to Skagway.

I stayed in Dawson awhile. I wanted to see Sarah who was as lovely as ever but in no hurry to marry a steamboat man.

A day or so after Christmas I started outside on the stagecoach. The first roadhouse we stopped at they had roast turkey for dinner and, from then on, twice a day roast turkey. If possible, I became more tired of it than the caribou.

That was a very fine stage line and all good roadhouses.

CHEECHAKO

Chapter nineteen

Barges

About March first of 1907, while in Seattle, Andy and I had to plan about moving a lot of lumber for barge material from Whitehorse to the foot of Lake Laberge.

Daub was in Seattle and had bought material for two barges, one large barge 36 x 150 and a smaller one. This he would ship to Whitehorse, and it was up to Andy and me to get it down to the foot of Lake Laberge, a distance of fifty-miles.

We bought three teams of horses and bob sleighs, hired two men, and loaded in Whitehorse soon after March first. Daub had shipped the lumber and it was almost in when we arrived.

Twelve miles below Whitehorse there was a deserted roadhouse which we planned to use. After a day in Whitehorse, we loaded the sleighs with lumber and our supplies. I drove one team and the men the other two. Andy came along to do the cooking for us, and he was good at it too. We had to break trail and so it was hard going. There was a lot of wind which drifted our trail full of snow, but we finally got the lumber all down on the lake. Daub came in with his crew and began building the barges.

All this time the weather was getting warmer, the snow almost all gone, and we could take down very large loads. A few miles from the foot of the lake the ice was getting soft so we had to make our teams trot to keep from breaking through.

Our last loads came down and at that weak place we had to get our horses on the gallop to make it. The last team and load went in anyway. The sleigh was loaded with lumber so could not sink and the horses kept their heads out of water. We unhitched the horses. We had a long length of strong rope on each sleigh which we tied to one of the horses and pulled him out on to solid ice with one of the other teams. After getting both horses out, we pulled the sleigh out with its load which was well tied to the sleigh.

We got down to where Daub was building the barges and found it was open water a hundred feet from shore—now what to do? We drove each team, after unhitching them from the sleigh, into the water and made them swim ashore. We then we pulled each sleigh ashore with its load—and was that a relief!

Daub soon had the barge ready. We loaded the horses and supplies on the big barge which Daub called "Bill." Daub floated it down the Thirty Mile River to where the Hootalinqua River comes in, and from there the White Pass Company would have one of their steamers make it over to Dawson. Captain Langley took the smaller barge down.

We sold two teams of horses in Dawson. I took one of the teams aboard the Tanana barge and went with the Tanana down to Chena but sold the horses at Rampart. Daub and Andy came down on a steamer that brought the big barge down to Tanana.

In Dawson I saw Sarah and she said, "You certainly are mixed up in the steamboat business". I told her some day I would quit and then we could get married.

Our crews had come from Seattle for the "Oil City" and "Crimmins" and we soon left for St. Michael. When our freight came in, we loaded the "Crimmins" barge first and she left for Fairbanks. Then we loaded the barges "Bill" and "Irene" each 400 tons and the "Oil City" 200 tons. We made it all right to Tanana. Now the steamer "Crimmins" had been up to Fairbanks and back to Tanana. She took some freight from each of our barges to lighten them for the Tanana River. So we made three successful trips the Summer of 1907.

After putting the boats and barges in the slough below Chena, Mr.

Daub and I were in Fairbanks getting our accounts settled up when the Alaska Commercial Company offered to buy us out. Daub and Dicky were in favor of selling, also Mersereaud & Clark, so we sold out and received a good price. All the freight money far more than paid for all the misfortunes we had.

CHEECHAKO

Chapter twenty

Vault Creek

After selling the boats and barges all my partners went out to Seattle. I stayed in Fairbanks, and a few weeks later met Tom McLain, the man who had helped me cut wood for my claim on Gold Hill in Dawson. Through him I met Bert Walker, a mining man. Bert and Tom knew of some mining leases to be had out on Vault Creek, some 20 miles from Fairbanks. Tom bought one lease and Bert and I the other.

So now I was mining again. This lease was on a creek claim and we had to build a cook and bunk house and a boiler house. It did not take long to do this. We installed a boiler and hoisting engine, hired two men, and started to sink a shaft which we knew would have to be 180 feet deep. My partner went to look after some other mining interests he had and I ran the hoist. The shaft was 8 x 8 feet and timbered all the way to bedrock. It was about the first of February, 1908, when we reached bedrock—found no pay, just prospects, so began drifting across the creek.

In March I became restless and thought about going to Dawson. I had Bert, my partner, come and run things and went to Fairbanks. I bought a small horse and basket sleigh and started for Dawson. The trail was good all the way and I had no trouble of any kind.

After coming up 400 miles to see Sarah, I found she did not seem at all glad to see me. About a week of this coldness and it got through my thick head that I was not wanted any more—in fact, that I had better go where I came from.

So I started back down the river to Forty Mile, on to Eagle and to Nation City where I stayed all night.

The day I left Nation the trail went close by a big bluff and just above this bluff my horse dropped into the river. Below these bluffs, against which the river runs, a big eddy formed, and this eddy had in some way prevented the ice from freezing thick. So the poor little horse was in the river with just his head out.

From past experience I knew what to do. I broke the thin ice in front of him to solid ice, but first I unhitched him. Now a horse in this situation will always keep his chin out on the ice. At the nearby shore I cut a good strong pole. Had to cut down a little tree and perhaps you don't think I hurried. I put one end of my prying pole under the horse, just back of his front legs, and with one good heave he had his front legs out on the ice. Then I put the pole just forward of his hind legs, gave another good heave and he was out and on solid ice.

I hitched him up again and found he was so cold he did not want to move—just stood there shivering. I had to get a good-sized willow and thrash him with it to get him moving. After getting him to trot slowly, he soon warmed up. All but his tail—it was frozen stiff.

Twelve miles below here there was a roadhouse at the mouth of a creek. That was our destination for the night. It soon became dark. When the horse came to a place where the wind had blown the snow off the ice, he would not cross it, so I took the axe and went ahead tapping the bare spots. The horse kept his nose very close to my back all the way to that road house.

At the roadhouse there was a nice warm barn with a stove in it—just what the horse needed. I also had a warm blanket for him.

The next morning the roadhouse keeper did not want me to leave—said it was too dangerous for me to travel alone. He wanted me to wait until someone else came along—which might be a long time. But I started on my way and made it to Circle City. From there the trail leaves the river, going overland to Fairbanks.

There was some new snow on the trail when we reached the foot of Eagle Pass. At one place the horse missed the trail and went down into deep snow. He was a very sensible horse and when I told him to be quiet, he just stayed still while I shoveled a way for him to get back to the trail. As I was wearing moccasins, and could feel the trail with my feet, I went ahead all the way up over the summit. I reached Fairbanks and sold the horse, which I hated to do, as we had become very fond of each other.

I became very restless at this time and as my partner did not need me anyway, I went on a hunting trip as soon as the Chatanika River opened. Vault creek emptied into the Chatanika a few miles below our claim.

CHEECHAKO

Chapter twenty-one

Fairbanks

I went back to Fairbanks and there I met a man I had known in Dawson. We bought a small boat and took it out to the Chatanika which was beginning to open. We stayed at the mine a week or so and then started down the river; just went along slowly, fishing and hunting ducks.

One day while walking around, a duck flew up at my feet. She had a nest with two eggs in it which I took back to camp. We cooked them in a little bacon grease and they were so very good, the best eggs I had ever eaten.

In passing near Lake Minto we went over and got some white fish from the Indians. We then drifted on down to the Tolovana River and went up that river for a couple of days.

My partner and I had agreed that if we saw a bear, I was to shoot it; if we saw a moose, he was to shoot it. On the second day, while rowing along, we did see a large moose standing on a bank not too far away. My partner grabbed his rifle, stood up in the boat, and fired away. The moose went into the woods and we after him but could not see anything. It is very difficult to shoot straight while standing up in a small boat.

That night we went a short distance up a small creek which flowed into the Tolovana and made camp. Next morning, hearing a noise where our boat was tied up, I got up in a hurry and, looking out, saw a black bear mauling things around in the boat. I got my rifle and took one shot at him. It was a lucky shot because it had pierced the heart. I told Will it must be a very old bear because I had noticed that his head was white or gray.

We found that he had torn open our flour sack, had been into the sugar and eaten some of the bacon. It took quite awhile to skin that bear. Neither one of us knew much about it.

We walked further up the creek and saw some beaver dams. The first I had seen, and very interesting.

Another day and we started down stream, camping that night in a nice place. In the evening we decided to go on down to the Tanana River and catch a steamboat for Fairbanks. There was a roadhouse and telegraph station just above the mouth of the Tolovana. We figured we would make it in a day. Got up early next morning and down at the water edge was a moose which my partner shot and killed—so now what to do? We could not kill a moose and leave it lay there, and our boat would not carry it. We made a raft and towed it down stream to Tolovana, and so it took us two days instead of one.

John Vachon, the roadhouse man, bought a quarter of the moose, which was all he could use. He told us the steamer Tanana was due upstream at any time and, sure enough, it came along soon. They were glad to get the rest of the moose. They took us and our boat free to Fairbanks.

I went out to the mine on Vault Creek. At the mine they had been drifting all the time but found no better pay. I talked it over with Bert, my partner, and we decided to quit and wash up our dump which was now thawed out. We rigged up sluice boxes, washed up the dump and got only half enough to break even. Later a man took over our claim and had only drifted eight feet further on one of the crosscuts when he found a rich pocket. He took out $15,000 in that one pocket. I guess that is the way things happen in mining.

Now I did not have either a mine or a steamboat. I stayed in Fairbanks all summer. That winter I went on a stampede down into the Hot Springs country, but found nothing after staking a claim and sinking a shaft to bedrock. So I went back to Fairbanks.

CHEECHAKO

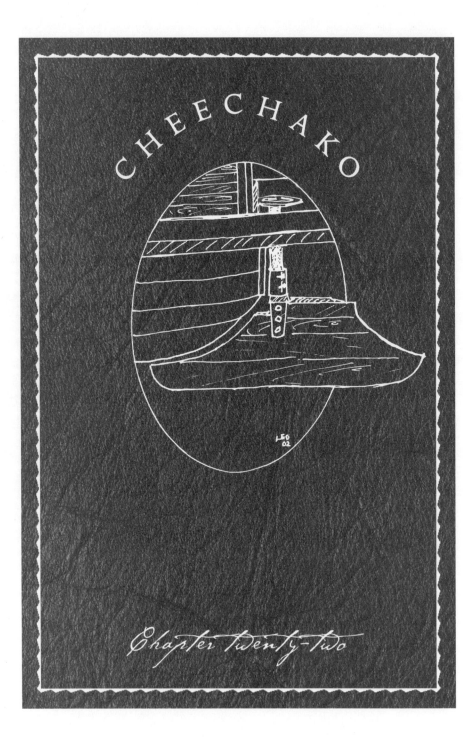

Chapter Twenty-Two

Elizabeth McComb

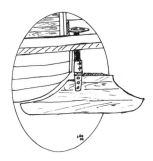

That fall the steamer "Julia B" came up to Chena. She was owned by some people in Illinois. In the spring of 1909, when starting for St. Michael, she took in tow a steamer without any machinery. Mr. McFarland had bought this steamer and wanted it taken to St. Michael where he had machinery to put into it. He hired me to go along as purser and pilot, Fred Lewis as chief engineer and Frank White as captain. He made arrangements for the "Julia B" to tow us down. I stood one watch on the "Julia B" and Captain De Pue the other.

One morning I was getting up to go on watch, when we came to a very sudden stop —throwing me forward against the wall. De Pue had gone to sleep or something, and the barge ahead of the boat went head on into a river bank. It hurt the bow of the barge some, but no other damage, and we made it all right to St. Michael.

When the machinery came in from Seattle, we had it installed. It was quite a job installing that machinery because so many things were missing. Now across the bay were a lot of abandoned river boats and when our Chief would need something, he would tell me and one of the crew to get into the work-boat and row over and get it. I remember one of the things I got was a steam whistle.

We were also having a barge built and McFarland had contracted for a load of freight to come up later on from Seattle. Well, our barge, the

"St. Paul", was finally built. Then we got all the machinery installed in the "Minneapolis". Our freight came in and loaded on the "St. Paul" and we were ready to start for Fairbanks.

Our Captain, Frank White, was a newcomer and did not know things around St. Michael; and about getting to the mouth of the Yukon he did not know the river either. When we were ready to leave St. Michael it was too rough to go around through Stephens Pass and White asked me to take the "Minneapolis" and barge through the Canal. I knew all about the canal, had been through it quite often. It is small and crooked and near the St. Michael end has some rocks in it. White said, "We can start now." I told him we could only start when the tide was coming in. Then, if we got on a rock or stuck any place, the tide would take us off.

We made it through the Canal without any trouble. The Canal is 16 miles long. It is shoal water at the end of the river and we started in when the tide was coming in half. After getting in and up a short distance, we tied up as we had great trouble in steering the boat. On examining the rudders, we found they were hung wrong—the longest part of the rudder was forward of the rudder stock, instead of aft. Had to take each rudder off and move the blade back. The blade should be about two-thirds aft and one-third forward. We again started up river and found that we could steer the boat without any more trouble.

It was after the first of September now. The nights were long and dark but much of the river I could run at night without a searchlight, which we did not have.

We made it to the mouth of the Tanana River. After considerable trouble we got into the mouth and on up to twelve miles below Chena where we found a shallow crossing which had not enough water to float our barge. We tied up and took some freight off the barge and put it on the steamer, got up over the crossing, put the freight ashore, then went back and took more freight off the barge. We did this four times. Then we reloaded the barge with the freight we had taken off and made it up to Chena and on to the freight train to Fairbanks.

The, "Julia B" by this time had come up from St. Michael with a loaded barge—got as far at Twelve Mile and could get no further. We received word that they wanted help so after putting our barge in winter quarters we went down to Twelve Mile.

The river was falling all the time and we got stuck for awhile. We finally reached the "Julia B" and took a load of freight off her barge to lighten it. Then found we could not get back over the crossing. We went back to the "Julia B," put the freight back on her barge, and put the "Minneapolis" in winter quarters in the mouth of Twelve Mile Slough. The "Julia B" and barge had to do the same. We left a watchman on each boat.

We walked up the river bank to Chena and took the train to Fairbanks. One of the first things I did was to go and see a very lovely lady, Elizabeth McComb, whom I had met several months before.

As purser of the "Minneapolis" I had quite a lot to do getting out freight bills and settling up the books and I want to say the owners of the "Minneapolis" were very much pleased to think that we had gotten up with all the freight. I must add, that, by this time, the rivers were all frozen.

It was October and I was seeing Elizabeth often. One day I asked her to marry me and she accepted. About the middle of October we were married. I had rented a nice cabin, in fact, a little house well furnished, and here we began our life together. Mrs. Robertson, the photographer and a great friend of Elizabeth's and a Mr. Henry Bloom, were the only two at our wedding. Mrs. Robertson gave us a nice camera and Henry gave us a three piece set of solid silver—a salad set I think —and I still have it.

CHEECHAKO

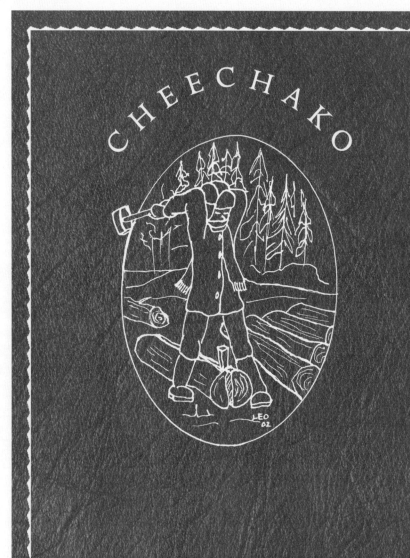

Chapter twenty-three

Twelve Mile

I could never stay idle very long and so the first of November got the silly notion of going down to Twelve Mile and cut cordwood for the river steamers. When I spoke to Elizabeth about it, she said it was all right with her—so down there I went.

There was a fine stand of spruce timber just below the mouth of Twelve Mile. I got the two watchmen off the "Julia B" and "Minneapolis" to help me build a cabin, and it did not take us long to build it either. We built a one-room log cabin in a few days, caulking the logs with moss with which the ground was covered. We had to make a fire and thaw it out.

When the cabin was ready, I went back to Fairbanks where Elizabeth and I got a lot of things together and on to Chena where I hired a dog team to take us to Twelve Mile. After getting settled we found it was a warm and cozy cabin.

I cut 50 cords of wood that winter and the two watchmen cut some, also. When we had cut all the timber that was handy, we hired a mule and sleigh from a woodchopper and fisherman who lived below us a couple of miles. We hauled and banked all our wood, helping each other.

It was too soon to go back to Fairbanks so I went down a short distance below and cut another 16 cords. One morning it was 65° below zero and the air very still. I heard two men talking on the trail a mile below and one said to the other, "that crazy fool must want cordwood awful bad to go out cutting in a cold day like this." It was cold—but wood split so easily in very cold weather. The trees were all frozen solid and just one blow with the axe would split a four-foot length easily.

The first of March came and I hired the mule and sleigh to take us up to Chena. I have a picture of that sleigh load with Elizabeth sitting on it.

We went up to Fairbanks and rented a house on Gordon Island which is just across the slough from Fairbanks. That spring, 1910 I guess it was, I hired out to go as pilot on the "Julia B." One of the owners was captain, another owner, Mr. Burrington, was purser, and Tom Youle, a part owner, was steward. Tom was an exceptionally fine man and a good steward. The "Julia B" had two barges which we loaded and started for the river. On the way up I had to do much extra work as the Captain did not know the river.

While I was away, Elizabeth had gone to stay with Mrs. Robertson who had living quarters above her shop. It was so good to get back and see my wife.

The time came very soon to go back after another load—so down again to St. Michael. While waiting for our freight, the Captain and Burrington got to quarreling about something and the Captain left us— got aboard a ship going to Seattle.

At that time I knew the river and steamboats better than most, but had neglected to get masters papers. We had to hire a captain who happened to be in St. Michael. This captain knew very little about the river and less about handling a boat—so I seemed to be always overworked. While in Fairbanks I went to see the steamboat inspectors who happened to be there and I got my masters papers.

I had a good friend in Tom Youle. One thing I remember about him was the *light* breakfasts he ate: a large bowl of mush, eight or ten slices of bacon, six eggs, toast and coffee. He was one of the best.

On our last trip up, the nights were long and dark so I stood watch from six in the afternoon until 6 A.M. We had a good searchlight along but I used it very little on the Yukon.

The Eskimos on the lower river called me "Owl-eyes man who could see in the dark." We reached Tanana and, after considerable trouble, made Chena. You must always expect trouble on the Tanana River in the fall.

While we were on our last trip, Elizabeth had gone out to Seattle to see her daughter, Florence. So I went out by way of Dawson, the way she had gone. We had put the "Julia B" and barges in the slough four miles below Chena for the winter.

CHEECHAKO

LEO
02.

Chapter Twenty-four

Ice

We stayed in Seattle until February and then as I had agreed to watch the "Julia B", especially during the breakup, we went to Valdez and over the trail to Fairbanks, then down to the "Julia B." I had left a watchman on her so let him go. We had a nice warm cabin there.

That spring I got a wire from the owners of the "Julia B" asking me to go on the "Julia B" as pilot with White as captain, and I refused.

It was then the Dominion Commercial Co. and Reagh & Peoples Co. bought the steamer "Minneapolis." They wanted me to go on her as purser and pilot, and I agreed.

Now the "Minneapolis" and loaded barge were lying at Dave Lewis' roadhouse, 30 miles above Ruby. She had been on her way to the Iditarod last fall and was frozen in. Right there the river is all in one channel and very little chance of saving her during the breakup. They had engineers, a mate, and a teamster, Champagne Bill, come to Fairbanks from Seattle.

We started for the "Minneapolis." We got as far as Tanana. There was no trail for horses from there to Dave Lewis' so I hired two dog teams to take us the rest of the way. There was the steamer and barge frozen in—right in the channel—and as much chance of saving them during the breakup as jumping over the moon.

The barge had to be unloaded so I started the men at that job. We put most of the freight in empty cabins.

That done, we cut a hole in the ice all around the boat next to the hull and almost to water. We sawed the remaining couple of inches all around and the boat was floating free of the ice. In the meantime, our cook had things going in the galley and we ate our meals on the boat. We had been eating at the roadhouse. We found a large cabin to sleep in.

I could see no way to save the boat and barge, other than to haul them out, and for this we would need at least three heavy blocks and tackles, and would have to sink deadmen. It would be a very big job and, of course, we had no such tackle.

I knew that up at Tanana there was such a tackle at the old Army Post so I started up river with the mail carrier. He had a fine dog team, and no trouble reaching Tanana. Sure enough, I was able to get what I needed and hired a man and dog team to take it down to the "Minneapolis", I went back with the mail carrier and on the way he asked me how I was going to save the boat. I told him what I thought of doing and he thought it a very big undertaking—and I did too.

In talking, he told me that when warm weather came, the river would start to rise and would come up an inch an hour; that the ice in deep water would rise with the water, but the ice next to shore would be frozen to the ground and would not come up until much later. He said there would be a narrow channel next to shore on top of the shore ice at least 3 1/2 feet deep before the ice let go and, that if I would have the boat and barge all ready, and steam up, I would move down stream and get behind an island two miles below.

Upon returning to the boat, I started the deck crew putting in deadmen and I took a walk down river. The head of an island was about a quarter of a mile down the river and a small channel off to the right, on the side we were on. The main river channel went to the left of the island, going down stream. As the small channel turned off to the right there was a large bluff that offered some protection. On down below that part of the island there was a rocky bluff sticking out with an eddy behind it that offered perfect protection if only I could get the "Minneapolis" there.

I went back to the boat and stopped the men digging to put in deadmen. On a boat the crew always refers to the Captain as the "Old Man". I heard some of the crew talking one day and one said, "What is the matter with the Old Man—he goes up there to get tackle to pull us out and now he is going to let the breakup wreck us."

Down here the ice does not get rotten or thawed before going out—it is all covered with snow and solid, as in the winter, when it moves. It is the great amount of water from above that takes it out. We had steam up now and all leaving aboard. I had all the wood, but a little, taken off and put on the barge to make the boat light as possible.

Old man river kept on coming up an inch-an-hour and we were all watching it. Another day and we were able to pull the boat and barge into shore. We, of course, were headed upstream.

The next afternoon we got started backing our way very slowly so as not to start the shore ice coming up. We made it down around the first bluff, when a big piece of ice came up between the boat and barge. There was nothing to do but tie the barge securely ashore and back down with the boat about halfway to where I wanted to go. There was a draw in the hills and out of it the wind had drifted a lot of snow. I thought we could back through it but just got stuck, and stuck hard—What to do now? Well, there was nothing we could do but wait for that inch-an-hour rise in the river to get us free.

That night I did not sleep—just paced the deck, watching the river. Next afternoon we were able to back on down to just above the point that I wanted to get behind. There had been a fish wheel installed. Now they had removed the wheel but left all the stakes there so some of the crew went down to get them out of the way. They just got there when a big piece of ice came loose from shore ahead of us. No time to wait now, and, calling to the men to get out of the way, I backed full speed down through all those stakes. Later the engineers said it sounded as if our wheel was breaking up. It did break one rudder and a few brackets.

We got below the point that jutted out and tied up just in time before all the shore ice came up. We were now as safe as if in dry dock, and, in several hours more the ice commenced to move and never stopped.

It is a wonderful sight to see—that ice moving and breaking up. Talk about an irresistible force—that ice was just that. They were saying up and down the river that the boat would be lost—that nothing could save her and word had gotten to Fairbanks that she was lost.

In a few days the ice was almost gone and we started upstream. We had to go to Tanana to pick up about 30 ton of freight that was coming from Seattle by way of Dawson. This freight consisted of fresh eggs and all kinds of fruits and vegetables for the miners in Iditarod

I crossed over to the opposite side of the river and up out of the Channel. At Ruby I sent Reagh & Peoples, the owners of the boat, a *long* telegram which said, "All O.K." signed Adams

We arrived in Tanana in August and Captain Borker came aboard. He had been hired by the owners to be Captain on the "Minneapolis." I had not told any of the crew about it and they were all surprised and disgusted.

We got our freight and then down to Dave Lewis to get the other freight. We picked up the freight I had put off and went on down to Shageluk Slough, going through it to the Iditarod River. The lower part of the Iditarod is low and flat and in the spring high watered—there being about five feet of water over it. We hired an Indian pilot to take us across the lower part and from there on the river is small and very crooked. We made it up to the town of Iditarod, discharged our freight and back to the Yukon and down to St. Michael. We picked up another load of freight and went back up to Fairbanks, then down and up again, and on down on our last trip of the season.

When we reached St. Michael, the steamer "Julia B" was there loading her three barges and she left about a day before we did. When we got to the mouth of the river the tide was out and over on the shoal part we saw that the "Julia B" was stuck. This seemed rather strange because at this time of the year we were having some of our highest tides. We had tide books which told us that a person should never try going in over the flats except when coming in so if they got stuck the incoming tide would float him off.

Captain White on the "Julia B" had started in at high tide, got out of the channel and stuck one of his barges, the other two he had tied up in the mouth. In passing the "Julia B" we stopped and asked Captain White if we could help him and he told us "No"—that he would just have to wait for the next high tide. So we went on.

I told Captain Borker, poor devil, there won't be another high tide like the last one until next January. We found out later that the "Julia B" had to unload one of the free barges and use it to lighten the stuck barge. That takes a lot of time and there is no time to lose on your last trip in the fall.

We, on the "Minneapolis," went on up to Chena and after unloading got a wire from the "Julia B" asking for help. She was now at Tanana. Our owner told us to go and help her. We went to Tanana, took one of her barges and brought it up to Chena. By that time the "Julia B" was about half way up. We went down and picked up another barge, took it to Chena, then back about 25 miles and took the last barge up over Twelve Mile, the last shoal place. Instead of bringing it on up to Chena, we tied it up, and the "Julia B" brought it the rest of the way.

I don't know how much the "Julia B" people had to pay the "Minneapolis" for all that work but it must have been a considerable amount.

We put the "Minneapolis" and barge down in the slough 4 miles below Chena for the winter. The "Julia B" also came in with her barges.

CHEECHAKO

Chapter Twenty-five

Julia B

I went up to Fairbanks for about a week. It was so nice to see Elizabeth. We got along so very well together. I had agreed with the owners of the "Minneapolis" to be watchman all winter, so my wife and I went down there. We had a nice cabin and had visitors several times that winter. There is very little to do watching the boats just take the snow off once in awhile. I did cut 16 cords of wood that was near the boats.

Once a week I would go up to Chena for our mail, Elizabeth walked up and back once. The spring of 1912, Dominion Commercial Co. and Reagh & Peoples Co. bought the "Julia B" and her barges and they asked me about going on her as Captain. Before a contract was signed they showed me a telegram they had received from Captain Borker who was in Seattle. This telegram did not praise me exactly and I could see that Reagh & Peoples were a little leery about hiring me. But they did, and needless to say, I did not engage Borker as pilot.

Anyway, now I was master of one boat and the other boat took their orders from me.

When it came time to start for St. Michael I figured I had to show Reagh & Peoples that I could handle a boat. When they asked me who I wanted for pilot I told them Hank Poles who lived up north of Seattle. I also told them to send him and the purser in on the ship that would bring our freight up from Seattle to St. Michael. This they did, and so I had a large steamer and four barges to take down all alone.

When I left for St. Michael, about the middle of May, Elizabeth went up to Fairbanks to stay with Mrs. Robertson. It seemed that we always had to be parting and each time it was harder than the last.

It was no fun taking four barges down the Tanana River. The Channel changes in so many places, but strange as it seems, we made it, and out into the Yukon where the Channel changes again—very, very seldom. All a pilot has to do is know where it is.

The only sleep I got that trip was when we tied up at a woodpile and we had to take on enough wood to take us from the mouth of the river to St. Michael and back to the mouth. We stopped at all the small towns on the way. At Nulato there is a Catholic Mission. Two of the nurses came aboard, wanting to go down to the Holy Cross Mission. I assigned them to the Captain's room, a nice large room; and I used the pilot's room for what little sleep I could get.

The "Julia B" was not a passenger boat, and so had very few passenger accommodations. When we got to Holy Cross I kept out of the way so the sisters could not find me. They wanted to pay their fare. The steward told them I was asleep and he would not dare awaken me. So they went ashore. There is a very fine Catholic Mission here at Holy Cross,

Now it was on down to the Bering Sea—had to wait in the flats a few days for the ice to clear out, then into St. Michael. The "Minneapolis" arrived a couple days later. Soon the ship with our freight came in. On it was our pilot and purser, and was I glad to see them.

Hank Poles was a very fine man, as well as a good pilot. We loaded the "Minneapolis" barge, mostly with fresh goods, potatoes, other vegetables and fruit and eggs, and started her up for Fairbanks where the load would be very welcomed.

Hank took charge of stowing the freight on our barge on one side, and our mate on the other. In four or five days we were on our way around through Stephens Pass and on to the mouth of the river. We were lucky in having good weather, as only then can you venture around and through the Pass.

Julia B

After getting into the river we stopped at an Eskimo village to take on wood. The natives catch drift-wood and cut it into cord wood. There are no trees at the mouth of the Yukon, not until you get about 300 miles up.

We got some wonderful king salmon from the Eskimos on our first stop. The finest salmon in the world.

CHEECHAKO

MINNEAPOLIS

Chapter Twenty-six

Freight

We went on up river. It is slow going with four barges and 1600 tons of freight. We had freight for many different places along the river which helped to lighten our barges. When we would reach the mouth of the Tanana River, which has many channels and not much water in any of them, it is almost always a very difficult task to get into the Tanana—and sometimes difficult all the way up.

It took us about 14 days to reach Tanana, but the "Minneapolis" with only one barge had been up to Fairbanks, left her barge, and was back to Tanana. She took one of our barges and started up again. We took one of our barges up into the mouth a short distance and tied it up, leaving a watchman on. Then we went back for the other two barges, and on up the river—two barges are all you can take up the Tanana.

We had quite a lot of freight for Hot Springs, about 100 miles up the Tanana. The store is four or five miles up Hot Springs Slough and only in high water could we take their freight right to the store. We tied the barge up at the mouth of the slough and I would take our small boat with a "kicker," and a man to run it, and go up the slough to sound it out. If I found enough water, we would take one barge and go up to the store. If not enough water, we would have to put their freight off at the landing three miles further up and they would have to haul it five miles.

We made it to Chena and while there we installed a big 65-foot-long

143

tow post in the center of the "Julia." This was to enable us to tow our barges astern in the Bering Sea, that is, from the mouth of the river to St. Michael, or from St. Michael to the river.

Sometimes, after getting our barges loaded and ready to go, the wind would be blowing and the sea too rough for our barges ahead of the steamer or alongside, and we often had to wait two or three days for the wind to quit. I figured that if we had a high tow post—high enough to carry the tow line clear of the wheel—we could tow the barges astern, having them one behind each other and about 20 feet apart. Then they would not bump into each other in rough weather.

I had the tow post come in from Seattle and we installed it—quite a job. We went to a drift pile up the Chena Slough, got two stout drift poles and rigged them up on the upper deck. We had a good carpenter aboard, also two good mates and a good crew, and so the tow post was installed without any difficulty.

I had also ordered a 6-inch manila hawser, 500 feet for a tow line. On the way down river the mates spliced six 20-foot lengths of cable, with eyes in each end, so they could easily be dropped over the tow posts on the barges.

Upon reaching the mouth of the river we had rough weather, so put our four barges astern, one behind the other, and started out. Everything went fine until we got through Stephens Pass—from there to St. Michael was the roughest stretch. A tow post on the third barge broke off. We had a man on each barge so he cast off and dropped anchor. We went on into St. Michael with two barges. The next day when the weather was better, we went back and picked up the other two barges.

I should have known that short stretch of cable between the barges would not work, as there is no give to cable. This time we made the same towing things but out of 6-inch manila line. When the barges were all loaded, we started out with them behind. After leaving the harbor, the barges would swing away out one way then back and out the other. We were just able to slowly get through Stephens Pass and drop anchor and get the barges ahead and alongside. Another crazy scheme of the Captain's was over. "What will our foolish Old Man try next," they all said.

Now the Dominion Commercial Company and Peoples were shipping all the freight that we could handle, which meant that our barges were very heavy to get into the Tanana River. All the traders along the way wanted us to carry their freight because, when checking their freight off, if they were short of anything, we would take whatever it was out of the Dominion Commercial Company or Peoples freight and give it to them. They liked that a lot better than checking them short and deducting it from what they owed.

Another important thing was that by putting off all that freight on the way up river, we had very little trouble getting in and over other bad places when we reached the mouth of the Tanana River.

I explained all this to Reagh & Peoples. They did not like it but they shipped some of their freight with the Northern Commercial Company and allowed me to take all the lower Yukon freight up to and including Tanana.

On this trip up we had brought material for a set of ways to be built at Chena, so that in the fall we could haul the boats and barges out giving them a chance to dry out and not become water-logged. Mr. Reagh knew of a good man whom he put to work building the ways.

Each trip up, the steamer "Minneapolis" would help us get into the Tanana and on up to Chena. On the way back to St. Michael, our last trip of the season (three trips being all we could make), I had our carpenter make two rudders to put on the stern of the last barge. When leaving St. Michael he also built a little pilot house on that barge.

I had another foolish idea that the stern barge had to be steered. We always kept a man on each barge anyway. In getting our freight off the ship, sometimes the weather would get bad, the wind making it so rough we would have to take our barges further up into the harbor, waiting until the wind let up, sometimes three days. We got loaded and our barges all astern and started out with the steering barge behind. He did not have to steer at all, he just put the rudders straight midship and they all came along like a string of box cars.

Now we could leave St. Michael in such bad weather that the other boats would not dare to venture out and this was very important, especially on the last trip of the season. Some of my Eskimo friends said, "Crazy Captain, him all right."

We would get on the flats at the mouth of the river, drop anchor when far enough to be safe, and rearrange our tow. Then when the tide was right, on up the river.

We burned a lot of wood in our boilers. We had the roof of each barge fixed so we could put about eight cords of wood on each barge, and the steamer with all the wood she would hold.

This season we had just a small crew on the "Minneapolis." She stayed at Chena, just coming down to the mouth of the Tanana to help us get up to Chena each trip.

Now we had a good set of ways and pulled everything out and jacked them up. We moved over to a nice large log cabin close to the ways, fixed it all up and Elizabeth and I stayed there all winter. I was watchman for the boats. The engineers, pilot and mates all went out to Seattle.

There were three other ladies in Chena that winter. Mrs. Ropp, Mrs. Belden and a missionary's wife, which made it nice for Elizabeth. We also had a telephone installed and that was good too,

I had very little to do—just keep the snow from becoming too heavy on the boats and barges, this required very little effort.

CHEECHAKO

Chapter Twenty-seven

Spring Launch

Spring came and time to launch. "Julia B" was the last to be launched and the owners came down from Fairbanks, also Mr. & Mrs. Suter. The man who directed the launching was certainly good at it and the "Julia B" slid into the water very beautifully. Then our visitors were served a nice lunch in our messhouse. Another successful trip to St. Michael with our four barges.

The Eskimos like seal oil, but only when it is old and rancid. They fill the empty sealskin with all its legs tied up, then hang it up in the sun until it is rancid and good—so they think. They catch those fine king salmon, dig a hole in the ground and put them it, then cover them up until they are *ripe* and good enough to eat. In the winter they cut a hole in the ice around the Bering Sea and fish for Tom cod. The fish freeze soon when thrown on the ice. Then, they take the fish into their igloos, pour some seal oil into a wooden bowl that they have carved out of a log, stand the fish up, slice it and dip it in the rancid oil and eat it. "Very good," so they say.

The Eskimos wear cotton parkas in the summer and never take them off—just let them rot and fall off, then put on another.

The beluga whales, which are white and about 8 feet long, come into the mouth of the Yukon. One was seen as far up as Tanana one time, but that is very unusual. They don't very often go up more than a couple of hundred miles.

When one of these whales is sighted at an Indian camp it is quite a sight to see the natives jump in their kayak, a skin canoe, and go after it with their spears. When they get one, what a feast they have eating the blubber.

At St. Michael, this first trip of the season, Florence, Elizabeth's daughter, came up from Seattle, on the ship with our freight. I had sent for her. She was a beautiful young girl with lovely blond hair. I think she was about 16 years old. She went up to Fairbanks with us, and late in the summer, back to Seattle by way of Dawson. This trip we made all right and on our next trip up I bought three dogs, a leader and two more—so that winter we had a dog team, even if it was a very small one.

The next year there was a boom on at Nenana, 60 miles below Chena. Elizabeth bought a lot there and, on our last trip down river, I took enough material to build a store building. After hauling our boats out that fall my wife and I went down there, hired a good carpenter and built quite a nice place. We came back to Chena and at the ways all the water was down again.

Next season the river was very low. We had a lot of trouble on the Tanana. On our last trip we tried several places before getting into the mouth of the Tanana. The steamer "Minneapolis" was there to help us and her Captain told me that the Tanana was bad all the way down. So we cached some freight and had the steamer "Tanana" take it up. After unloading at Chena we found that the river was so low we could not get up on our way. We went down to the steamboat slough and could not get in there. Nor would we get in at Twelve Mile Slough. Then we went down to a slough about 14 miles below Chena and got in there.

We had taken enough lumber along to build a nice cabin and Elizabeth and I were there for the winter. We were lucky that we had the little dog team so we could go up to Chena once in a while.

After getting settled, I built three nice warm doghouses. They had double flooring with building paper between each and a small door with a canvas flap which would close after they went in. I also put quite a little hay inside them. I tied each dog to his house, and when the first cold weather came, thought they would go inside but they did not—just curled up on the snow or on top of the house. They were huskies and had thick warm fur.

We always kept our dogs tied up, otherwise they would roam around and get to fighting. They would rather fight than eat. They would always jump on the dog that was down, and if there was four or more, a dog would grab each end of the down dog, stretch it out, and the third dog would rip the dog's belly open, killing it.

We had a good winter here—I think it was 1917 by this time. In the spring, before breakup time, our crews came from Seattle to get the boats ready for the breakup. We had steam up on each boat, with the crews standing by. The ice began moving in the Tanana, which did not bother us any, but then it jammed above the mouth of our slough, which raised the water and forced the ice all down our slough. I moved the "Julia B" over to the other side, which was a bad mistake, as the "Minneapolis" and barges stood it all right on the deep side. The jam finally let go out in the river, dropping the water, and I made another mistake—did not watch close enough and got caught on the shoal bank.

We ran a cable over to the deep side, not very far, the "Julia B" bow slid out easy enough, but the wheel had settled on some blocks of ice and would not budge. We hurriedly cut away about a fourth of the wheel, then with the bow cable, and one in the stern, we pulled the "Julia" into deep water and to the other side. You see the water was dropping and we had to hurry and get the "Julia" into deep water.

After the ice was all gone we took the "Minneapolis" and a barge up to Chena for some wheel material and another carpenter, and soon had the "Julia's" wheel all fixed.

Each spring, on our first trip to St. Michael, the "Minneapolis" and barge would come along, get a box of fresh goods as soon as possible, and take them to Fairbanks where they would be gladly received after a long winter without fresh provisions. We made our three trips that season, always towing our barges astern from St. Michael to the mouth of the river. That fall the White Pass Co. took over all the steamboats on the lower river including the "Julia B" and "Minneapolis" and barges.

CHEECHAKO

Chapter twenty-eight

1918 Season

Elizabeth and I spent the winter in Seattle, and in the following spring, 1918, I was hired by the White Pass Company and went into Whitehorse. Elizabeth stayed in Seattle. Each parting always seemed harder than the last.

In Whitehorse I was put in charge of the steamer "Alaska," a very fine passenger boat. We had a full load of passengers, including our mate's bride, our first engineer's bride, and a mining man with his bride from the Fauber country. Our first engineer's name was Dow and the other mate's name was Buckholtz who now lives in Long Beach, California.

We left Whitehorse when we thought Lake Laberge would be open but it was not. After a couple of days the ice did become rotten enough so that we could shove through it and on to Dawson, then down past Forty Mile, Eagle, Circle City, Ft. Yukon, Rampart, Tanana and up the Tanana to Fairbanks.

Two miles above Hot Springs, on our second trip down the Tanana River, we stopped for wood. I had gone off watch at noon and was asleep in my room when I awakened, feeling very sick; felt as though I wanted to vomit very badly, got up out of my bunk and fainted. I happened to lie with my head near the door, which was partly open. and the steward going by, saw me through the screen door. He called the pilot and they found a lot of blood in my room. I had a hemorrhage of some kind.

They put me in my bunk. The pilot, Horace Loomy, took the boat down to Hot Springs where our agent, Ernie Barstow, got the doctor at the Army Post into a fast launch and started him up river. In the meantime, the "Alaska" was headed down river. When I came to, the doctor was giving me a shot in the arm. At Tanana the crew carried me off on a stretcher to the Army hospital. The doctor took good care of me. He thought I had an ulcer of the stomach, and he was right.

Elizabeth, who was then at Nenana, came down and in ten days the doctor let me go to the roadhouse where Elizabeth was staying. In another week we went aboard the "Alaska" on her way up to Dawson. The White Pass Superintendent gave me two pilots for the rest of the season. After another trip Elizabeth stayed in Nenana. I made a couple of more trips and left Chena for Dawson, on our last trip, on the last day of September at 10 P.M., 1919. We had a full load of passengers and five empty barges to take down to the mouth of the Tolovana River for the winter.

Leaving Chena on this last trip, our purser had placed a very beautiful lady, Mrs. St. George, and her small son, Harry, at my table, next to me. The steamer "Alaska" had a very fine dining room with eight tables. John Vachon, the store and roadhouse keeper at Tolovana had a few goats, and knowing that I had stomach trouble, would give me some goat's milk. It would help me a lot. It was very nice of him to do so. Some of the milk I gave to Mrs. St. George's son who did not eat much and was rather thin.

It was long after dark when we left Chena and the river was very low. We had to back down just below a bluff to turn around—and barely had room to do so. We had a searchlight and got along fine over a lot of shoal places. I finally got stuck one place but was able to work off without running a line.

Daylight came and we made it to Nenana where we picked up another barge to put in winter quarters. We got the barges down and tied them up in the mouth of the Tolovana, then on down river. It seemed so good to be free of those barges.

We reached the mouth of the Tanana before dark on September 2 and the ice had started to run. After sounding around we were able to make it into the Yukon River. At Tanana we had to pick up a large mail launch for Dawson. We tied it alongside the "Alaska" and went on up to Rampart and into the Yukon flats, a long stretch of river that is all split up into many channels and not much water in any of them.

The ice was running a little heavier all the time and had commenced to damage the mail launch. We stopped and put a good-sized log along side the launch to fend off the ice, then on up past Ft. Yukon which is just inside the Arctic Circle. There, on the longest day of the year, we could see the sun at midnight.

We reached Circle City and left the mail launch to be hauled out onto the bank. We had to pick up a couple of barges to put into winter quarters a short distance up the river. This we did and started up with the steamer alone. The ice was running heavier and heavier all the time and soon it began to cut into the bow and sides of the steamer. So we tied the steamer up to a sloping bank. We got some space buffer planks and nailed them on at the water's edge. We turned the boat around, nailed planks on the other side, and went on again.

Going back up river above Circle, after nailing the planks on the sides of the boat, we got along all right until we reached Cliff Creek, 12 miles below Forty Mile, where the river was down against a high bluff, and very narrow—so narrow that the ice was running very thick there and we could not got through it. Our steamer would push her way only a short distance when the ice would stop her and then take her back down stream with our wheel going full speed ahead. After trying it a few times we drifted back and tied up as it was dark. We figured we would have to run a cable up above the bluff and that could not be done in the dark.

Next morning we moved over to just below the bluff and tied up. Some of the crew went up over the bluff with a small line, and on getting down above the bluff, tied one end of the line to a piece of driftwood. They put it in the edge of the river and we caught it down below and tied it to a strong, long cable. The men above pulled it up and fastened it to a deadman which they had put in. Now we were all ready to try to get up above the bluff. We attached the cable to the stern of the boat. The Captain started and went along for a very short distance when the cable broke and the ice took us back.

After getting all our men aboard we went over to the opposite side of the river and tied up. It looked very bad for us now. We had 150 passengers, and if caught here for the winter, they would have to get up to Eagle, somehow. It would not be too hard for most of the men, but for elderly men, the women and the children, it would be hard to go through the woods and brush and climb over the hills.

I started the deck hands cutting wood for our boiler again, and could do no more. The weather kept very cold and the ice was getting thicker.

The next day the steamer "Seattle" came along on her way to Dawson. They went full speed into the ice at the bluff, went ahead a few feet, then, with her wheel going ahead full speed, she stopped and was pushed back down the river. She came over and tied up below us.

Now every morning, at daylight, I would go up to the pilothouse to look at the barometer. The morning after the "Seattle" came along, when entering the pilothouse, I saw one of the finest things that I could ever hope to see. The barometer had dropped away down low, and I knew a change was due in the weather. By afternoon a Chinook wind began to blow from the southwest and soon the ice commenced to thin out. Another day and we got started and made it up past the bluff. The "Seattle" was also getting through.

The "Alaska" could travel faster than the "Seattle" but I made our pilot follow close behind her. I knew our hull would not stand too much ice cutting into it. The hull of the "Seattle" was covered with iron sheathing and the ice did not bother her, so we followed her all the way to within a few miles below Dawson where we passed her, and in ahead to Dawson.

I forgot to say that on the morning we got through at Cliff Creek, I had the steward see that all the passengers were up and dressed. I did not know just what might happen. We might have gotten half way past the bluff and then shoved back by the ice and against the bluff, which would not have been so good. But now we were at Dawson—and what a relief! The ice was thinning out and the weather good.

We were in Dawson a few hours in the afternoon and left that evening, the Company putting an up river pilot aboard. A lot of our passengers were celebrating. At Dawson they had brought aboard a lot of something that was not exactly water—something they could not do in Alaska.

On up the river, and above Selkirk, there was no more ice—and a good thing as our poor hull was worn very thin by this time.

We finally reached Whitehorse late one afternoon and there would be a train leaving for Skagway the next morning. Our passengers more than filled the hotels, and I told Mrs. St. George and some others to stay aboard that night.

CHEECHAKO

Chapter twenty-nine

Illness

In a couple of days I and our crew left for Seattle. On reaching Seattle
I went directly to Mayo Brothers Clinic in Rochester, Minnesota. I was
examined and sent to a hospital for an operation. They told me I had a
duodenal ulcer.

I got along fine after the operation but they would only let me stay
ten days in the hospital. They needed the room so I went to a hotel—ate
the wrong thing that evening and become very sick during the night. I
went down to the lobby and phoned a doctor. He said for me to take
some soda. I asked the clerk to get me some and went up to my room
and took it. Then I was really sick. It was not soda—it was cream of tartar.
I went to the clinic the next day and they washed out my stomach and
sent me to a convalescent home where I had the right food and was fine
from then on.

After a couple of weeks I went down to New Orleans—thought it
would be warmer there. I seemed to feel the cold so much. I did not like
it in New Orleans and went to New York for the winter. I thought it
would be too cold for me up in Nenana.

While in New York the winter of 1919-1920, I attend a School of
Photography just to pass the time away. I like Grand Opera and I heard
Caruso sing more than once at the Metropolitan Opera House. Also
heard other great singers.

Spring came and I went to Seattle. I got orders to go to St. Michael. I left Seattle the 8th of June 1920 on a freighter and arrived at St. Michael the 16th. I was given the steamer "Seattle" which had just come down from Dawson.

We loaded two barges with freight and on up the river. I wired Elizabeth to come downriver to meet me, and this she did, arriving at Ruby just as we did. It sure was wonderful to be together again—but not for long. She stayed at Nenana on our way up to Chena.

I told Elizabeth to sell our place in Nenana and she did. She came down to St. Michael on my next trip, and out to Seattle.

Now the upriver boats had brought down the Stewart River five barge-loads of ore, silver and lead. I got orders to take them down to St. Michael to be shipped to Seattle. We took them all in tow, 2000 tons, and started down the river.

On the trip Volney Richmond was a passenger as far as Ruby. This was in 1921 and he was forming a new company to take over the old Alaska Commercial Company stores. He was getting the agents at the different stores, and others, to take stock in the new Alaska Commercial Company. Mr. Richmond wanted to stop and see a mail carrier 20 miles below Tanana. We could not stop, only in certain places, with that heavy tow, so we just drifted slowly past the mail carriers' place, blowing our whistle and calling to him to come alongside. He got into his small boat and came alongside one of the barges where Mr. Richmond could talk to him. He promised to take stock in the new company, and I did also.

We had mail to deliver at all the small towns and as we could not stop, we would just drift along above each place. The purser would get into our workboat with the mail, taking along a man to deliver the mail, and then catch up with us.

As far as I know that was the heaviest tow ever to go down the river. It was all daylight at this time so we got along fine down to the mouth of the river and out on the flats where I had orders to turn the barges over to another steamer.

On our last trip that season we went back to St. Michael, where the boats and barges were hauled out for the winter. Leaving St. Michael, the "S.S. Victoria" went over to Nome to put off some freight and to take aboard a lot of passengers going outside for the winter. This was the year that bad sickness was around—influenza, I guess it was. Anyway, it was bad and on the way to Seattle several of the passengers died. Some were buried at sea and others were put in cold storage.

Leaving Nome we crossed the Bering Sea through the Pass and out into the wide and deep Pacific—only it was not very pacific—we got into a terrible storm the first night after leaving the Pass.

The "Victoria" was a fine built ship, built in Scotland 60 years ago, and she did not hesitate any when it came to rolling.

The purser and the pilot of my crew were in the room with me. I was on the lower bunk when a big wave came along and smashed open our door and window and, of course, I was covered with water. Our ship was getting into the storm's path and the Captain had to change course and run head on into it for three days. I got up and dressed the night the wave broke in. It also smashed in the door of the room next to ours, and a man and his wife were scared to death. We went into the smoking room and for the rest of the night sat around a steam radiator to dry out. Every time the ship would roll, the rail would go under water. To get to the dining room, which was aft, we would watch when our side came up and then make a run for it. In the dining room there would only be 6 or 8 people. The tables and stools were bolted to the deck, and each table had a little railing around it so the dishes could not slide off to the floor. One had to hang on with one hand and eat with the other. It seems to me Captain North was master of the "Victoria" at the time.

The storm finally quit and we reached Seattle. All the people on the dock who had come down to meet us were wearing something over their mouths and noses.

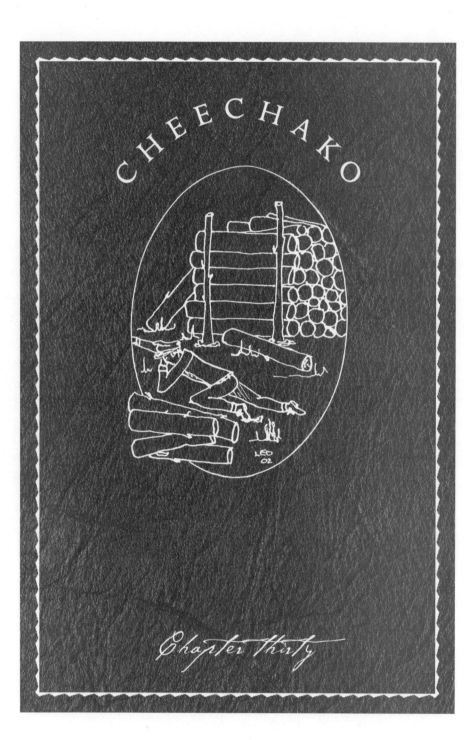

CHEECHAKO

Chapter Thirty

Alice

Elizabeth was on the dock to meet me and we stayed in Seattle all winter. The following spring she stayed in Seattle while I went to Whitehorse and on the "Alaska" again. We went down to the Stewart River and made a few trips up to Mayo to bring down ore, and then on the run between Dawson and Fairbanks before going out to Seattle for the winter.

In Seattle, that fall, we bought a car and made a trip down to Los Angeles, San Diego and back. While down there we bought a lot in Santa Monica. That summer, 1923, Elizabeth stayed in Seattle. I went up again for the White Pass Co.,—up and down the river. All this time the U.S. Government was building the Alaska Railroad.

Late that fall I was told to take the steamer "Tanana" whose tow had gone outside, and take two barges down river to put in winter quarters in the mouth of the Tolovana River. On the way back we were going along, about 11 P.M., up a narrow shoal channel at Minto. I was on watch, and at this point, felt an awful jarring commotion. It was caused by the steamer striking a rolling submerged stump with roots which had dropped in the river from up above some place where they had been cutting wood.

It tore a big hole in the bottom of the "Tanana" under the boilers, and she sank in a few minutes. The water was only a little over three feet deep. We had no way of raising her, so next day built a log cabin ashore for a watchman. The rest of us walked up to Nenana.

The next spring, before the ice went out, the boiler was moved ashore and anything else that was worth-while, and she was let go with the ice. That winter the Company wrote me a nice letter saying that the "Tanana" was old and worn out anyway.

I believe it was 1923 when the Alaska Railroad was finished with a bridge built over the Tanana River at Nenana and President Harding drove the Golden Spike just across the bridge at Nenana.

Now the White Pass Company quit the lower river run as there would be no more freight coming upriver—it would come in on the railroad and go downriver. The White Pass Company still had a boat on the Dawson run; the Alaska Railroad took over the Army's two river steamers—the "Jeff Davis" and the "Jacobs." They hired me to run the "Davis" and we made a trip down to Marshall and returned every two weeks—the "Jacobs" doing the same. In the fall the boats and barges wintered at Nenana while the crews went out on the railroad to Seward and on the ocean boats to Seattle.

After a couple of years the Alaska Railroad thought they would build a large river steamer to take the place of the two small ones and it could be run with one less crew. So they got to work on it.

The steamer "Jeff Davis" was very old and so one fall they hauled her off the end of the ways. Then I was given the steamer "Alice" to run. She was light draft and much better on the Tanana River, but one season, while moving a few miles above Nulato she broke her shaft. We were able to tie up and then sent the purser down to Nulato in a small boat so he could send a wire to our Superintendent, Cunningham. He instructed the "Jacobs" to help us on her way down.

We all went aboard, leaving a watchman on the "Alice." Below Holy Cross we got off at the mouth of the Shageluk Slough with two small boats, and then, over to the Iditarod River where we leased a small river steamer and barge. With her we made two or three trips until the "Alice" was tied up to Nenana and a new shaft and wheel installed. We finished out the season all right.

ALICE

That winter Elizabeth and I went down to Santa Monica and had a house built on our lot—quite a nice house. In the spring Elizabeth stayed there while I went north and back on the "Alice."

About the middle of the season, on our way upriver to Ruby, I was off watch and had turned in, but not asleep yet, when I heard the pilot, Hollis Looney, blow the whistle to cast off leaving Ruby. After leaving, he stopped the engines—then went ahead—then stopped again. Thinking something was wrong, I got up and went to the pilot house. On going in, Hollis never looked at me he was just steering around and would ring to go ahead, then stop. I asked him what was wrong and he never answered—so I shoved him aside and took over. I rang for the mate and he took Hollis to his room. He had a stroke of some kind. Now I had to stand the pilot's watch and my own also. I would sleep while taking on wood, and the mate would steer in some of the good places. I was fifty some hours in the pilot house. We sent Hollis to the Company doctor in Anchorage. I made another trip, sleeping only at woodpiles and while putting off freight. Bill the mate, helped out.

Next trip, and our last for the season, Hollis was back and apparently all right. Do you know, nobody could make him believe that he had anything the matter with him. On our way back, about 12 miles above Koyukuk, the river was very high on account of a lot of rain and had covered any low places. Just above a bluff there was such a low place, and about 2 A.M. the pilot, Hollis Looney, got on this flat and the steamer got stuck. I heard bells ring again and got up to find the steamer was stuck. The barge being much lighter, was not aground and it just happened that there was no place to fasten a line to that would help us off. We got the spars out and tried to spar off, but no good. All the time we were working, poor Hollis was up in the pilot house ringing bells. I had told the engineers not to answer any bells. You know, I was to blame for leaving Hollis alone in the pilot house.

Daylight came and I sent a small boat down 12 miles to Koyukuk with a wire to our superintendent. The next morning the steamer "Jacobs" came down to help. We were very lucky that the river did not fall. If anything, it rose a little.

The "Jacobs" came alongside, tied up to our steamer and we went ahead full speed—but no good. Then the "Jacobs" tied up to our barge in such a position that her wheel would wash under our boat, and in two hours she washed us free. We got into the river and from there on to Nenana I did not let Hollis in the pilot house. Same old grind for me—sleep at the woodpiles and have the mate steer in good places on the Yukon, but on the Tanana I stuck it out myself and we did not go aground anywhere.

That winter poor Hollis had a stroke and passed away.

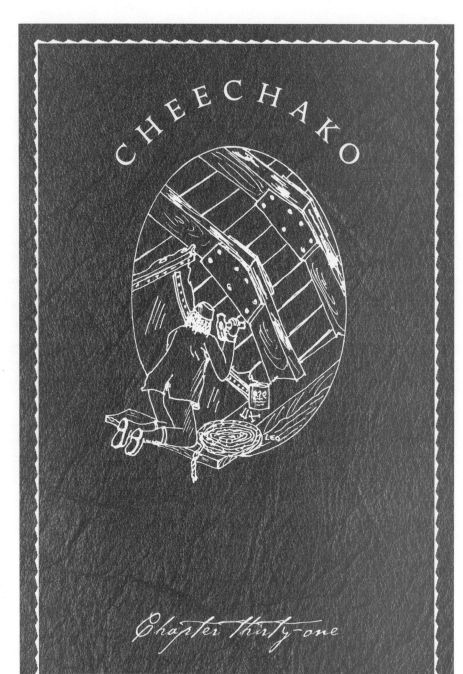

CHEECHAKO

Chapter thirty-one

Nenana

I spent the winter in Santa Monica. In the spring I went to Nenana and had an uneventful season until the last trip up river. The river was very low and cold weather had set in. We got into the mouth of the Tanana, and up near Hot Spring, when the ice started to run, it kept getting thicker and thicker until about six or eight miles above Hot Springs. We could go no further, and stopped at the mouth of Dugan Creek.

We built a log cabin for a watchman, and the rest of us started walking up to Nenana. There was a roadhouse at Dugan Creek so we all had a good breakfast and then started for Tolovana, the next roadhouse, about 30 miles. We were a very tired lot of men when we reached Tolovana late that evening. It always seems so good to get into a roadhouse after a hard day's walk. I remember all had moose steak for dinner that night.

The next day we got to a roadhouse at Minto, another 30 miles. Another roadhouse the next night, then to Nenana and we were through walking—could now ride the train to Seward and on to Seattle. I was going to Santa Monica, and those homecomings were always so wonderful.

Next spring back to Nenana, and there was word around that the "Alice" had been left right in the Channel and could not be saved when the ice went out.

We reached Anchorage and our Superintendent asked me if there was danger of the "Alice" being lost during the breakup. He also had heard that she could not be saved. I told him that I had saved boats in worse places than she was in, that I had left her there because it was a good place, and that he could forget about her. He said, "I do not understand it but I am going to do just that."

Reaching Nenana, we had a couple of dog teams take us down to the "Alice." We stayed at the roadhouse several nights until the engineers got steam up and the cooks got things started—then moved aboard.

The first thing to do was to cut a trench all around the boat and barge, next to the hulls, almost to the water, then saw the rest. We were right at the mouth of Dugan Creek which I knew would open up a few days before the river did. I also knew that the river would have to rise eight feet before the ice would move, and that the shore ice would not let go until just before the main ice moves; that there would be plenty of water on the shore ice for us to go up into the mouth of the creek, but that we must have steam up and be watching and waiting.

Warm weather came and the river commenced to rise and we commenced measuring the depth of water on the shore ice every hour or so. In a day or two more, I guess, we measured it every few minutes. Then came the time when there was enough water and I went up to the pilot house, rang the ready signal to the engineer, and when they answered "ready" we just went ahead up into the mouth of the creek— going up about a quarter of a mile. In a few hours, we watched the break-up; and if we had not moved, the ice would certainly have smashed us to bits.

On the lower Yukon it takes almost a 20-foot rise to take the ice out as it does not thaw any before moving, while on the Tanana River the ice thaws quite a little before moving. In a few days the ice was all gone and we started for Nenana. There were a lot of surprised people on the way up and at Nenana.

Soon it was time to start downriver again with a barge load of freight. Most of our freight was put off at Holy Cross. We had a warehouse there and an Agent. This freight was taken up the Iditarod River with small boats to the mining camp of Iditarod. We finished the season and out home where I found Elizabeth had become quite ill. That summer she went to the Mayo Brothers. I was back in Nenana and found they had started to build the new steamer "Nenana".

That fall, the steamer "Jacobs," on her last trip down, was badly stuck just below Tolovana. We were all through, but received a wire for help so went down there with our empty barge, and found the "Jacobs" had taken the wrong channel and her loaded barge was hard aground. We took enough freight off to lighten it and when afloat, tied it up in deep water, then put the freight back.

We then went back to Nenana and outside. Arriving home in Santa Monica, I found Elizabeth was very ill and the next summer she came up to Nenana with me, thinking the trip might help her. At Nenana Mr. & Mrs. Donald asked Elizabeth to stay with them, which was a wonderful thing for them to do. Jack Donald was agent for the Northern Commercial Co. They had a lovely house.

This season was finished all right; but at home that winter Elizabeth kept getting worse, and she passed away the latter part of March. A terrible shock to have a loved one go, and she was one of the finest women in the world.

I went back to Nenana and was put on as master of the new steamer "Nenana" which they had just finished. Only one crew now and only one boat. But we kept the steamer "Alice" in commission to help, if needed, and lucky we did as the "Nenana" was way too deep at the stern and could not be handled right in shoal water. That fall we had to split crews, my pilot, Livingston, taking the "Alice" and I the "Nenana" alone.

There is a lot of freight in the fall and in this way we got it all down. That winter we had new rudder stocks made for the "Nenana"—the old ones were much too long and were solid steel, so were very heavy. The new ones were of hollow steel and much shorter. We also put in new log posts and chains which helped lift the stern when launched. She sat just right in the water and could do what a river boat should do.

On our second trip down, near the mouth of the river, our barge struck a lump very hard, but did not got stuck—just flattened it out—

but the jar started a leak in the bow of the "Nenana." We were quite close to shore, so tied up, and were able to stop the leak with oakum and canvas. We found the bow had not been built right, and we would be unable to tow our barge ahead.

At this time, the mouth of the Tanana was very shallow and difficult, and we could never make it with the barge alongside—so what to do? It looked like an impossible situation until just then we heard a steamboat coming up the river. It was the White Pass steamer "Yukon," on the Dawson-to-Fairbanks run.

Captain Ralph Newcomb, whom I know very well, was aboard, and I asked him to take our barge down to the Yukon. This he proceeded to do and we followed him with the "Nenana." At this time the Channel at the mouth came out four miles below Tanana, and he tied up our barge there. That was a very fine thing for Captain Ralph to do. Once in the large and deep Yukon River we could get along fine with the barge alongside. Before leaving, we sent the purser to the town of Tanana to wire our superintendent to send us material, and a carpenter to fix our bow.

We went on down the river and were half way back to Tanana when the carpenter came in a launch and had our bow fixed up before we got to the Tanana River.

The freight shipments were always heavy at the last of the season, so again we split the crew, Livingston taking the "Alice" and I alone, the "Nenana." At Louden, on our way up the last trip, we encountered a very heavy down-stream wind. It blew so that we could make only a mile an hour, sometimes, but we did make 30 miles that day, reaching a woodpile late evening, tying up for the night and taking on a lot of wood. The wind died down in the night.

Speaking of wind, one trip up with the "Julia B" and four loaded barges, we got in a bad wind storm 60 miles up from the mouth. We were half way up a long bend when it got so rough our tow was in danger of breaking up. This was about 10 P.M. and dark. We could not tie up in that rough bend, so I headed across the river into shoal water—nothing to tie up to and our anchors would not hold in such a wind. So I rammed the bows of the two head barges against a sand bar, then stopped the engines, and, the wind started to blow us back. We had to shove these barges very hard against the bend and this time the wind could not blow us away.

The next morning, after the wind let up we had to do a lot of backing to get free. At St. Michael that night they said the wind blew 70 miles an hour and it blew some shingles off the roofs.

CHEECHAKO

Chapter thirty-two

Helen

Another season finished and I came out to Santa Monica where I had a nice apartment for my sister Mary, who had come from Minneapolis, and Florence to live with me. That winter, while downtown one day, I met Mrs. St. George. It was very nice to see her again, and she was still as beautiful as ever. I saw her several times before going north. Her husband had died at Juneau, Alaska, on his way out, some three or four years earlier.

I went north again next spring—had a good season and back home. That winter I saw Helen (Mrs. St. George) quite often. Along in the spring I asked her if she would like to go to Alaska. She said, "What would I go to Alaska for?" I told her I knew a man who would like to take her there. She looked at me a moment and then said, "Are you the man who wants to take me?" When I said I was the man, she replied, "Well, for being so smart, I will go." So we were engaged and on April 12, 1933, we were married at Mrs. Emily Sleight's home in Santa Monica. Mrs. Sleight was a niece of mine.

We had a very nice wedding and left that evening on the train for Seattle, going by way of Salt Lake City where my nephew lived with his mother and sisters. A couple of days there and on to Seattle for a week before going to Nenana—a wonderful trip! At Nenana we were able to rent the Northern Commercial Co's house, the Donald's having gone outside. There were a number of ladies in Nenana at that time and some at the Mission. Then Helen could go up to Fairbanks on the train when she felt like it.

On our second trip down it became very foggy above Ten Mile and I should have tied up, but very foolishly thought I could let the boat and the barge just drift over the crossing. So I headed in the right direction, stopped the engines, and called for soundings. There was no bottom—no bottom all the time, but we did not get across the river. I told Bill, the mate, to go and see about the soundings and he found the men sitting down and calling out "no bottom" without sounding. When Bill put a pole down, he found we were not moving. We were stuck, so there we stayed until the fog lifted. We then had to run a cable and pull ourselves off.

On our way back from this trip, 15 miles above Marshall, something broke in one of our engines. We sent the purser down to Marshall to send a wire to our Superintendent, and when the purser came back we came on up the river with one engine. Mr. Kinsil came down in a launch, meeting us before we got to Tanana. He had the necessary parts and we were soon on our way with both engines working.

We finished the season without any more trouble, and that winter rented an apartment in Los Angeles. In the spring it was back to Nenana. Those trips were all very enjoyable. No trouble on the river, and out again to Los Angeles where we had a nice car and drove around a lot—up to the Grand Canyon and other places.

Next season while at Nenana, one morning we found my pilot, Livingston, dead in his bunk—heart trouble. He was a heavy drinker and I had to stand his watch more than once.

Now I would take the "Nenana," alone, down to the Yukon and then Howard, my nephew, and Bill, the mate, could steer a lot. Had no more trouble except the usual trouble of getting in and out of the mouth of the Tanana River.

Outside again for the winter, and then back to Nenana. That season our purser, while going from the dock to the station house at Nenana, dropped dead—another case of heart trouble. He was a very fine man.

They had a man come in to go pilot with me from the Columbia River. I still had to take the boat down the Tanana, but once in the Yukon, Howard could show him the way. So that season was finished.

The mining camps were getting worked out, all placer mining, so there was not much freight for Hot Springs, Ruby, Iditarod and Marshall. The season went along fine until the last trip up with the "Alice." She was able to handle all the freight, but we were late and the weather cold. Below Hot Springs the ice was running and getting thicker. We wanted to get into the mouth of Hot Springs Slough but could not make it. We turned back, 15 miles or so, to Crossjacket, an Indian Camp. There was a slough there which I knew we could get into, and we did, getting in out of the river ice. At that time we had a wireless set on the "Alice" so wired our Superintendent. He wanted to know if an airplane could land near us and, if so, in two days he would have one pick us up and take us to Nenana. It so happened that there was a high flat bar near us, covered with small willows and weeds, and we easily cleared it off and planted a large white flag at one side. We wired Nenana what we had done, and on the second day the airplane came. We left a watchman on the "Alice" and the plane took us to Nenana in two trips.

Helen and I came out to Los Angeles, and my beautiful niece, Irene, and her husband, Dr. Thomson; always invited us to stay with them until we found an apartment.

CHEECHAKO

Chapter thirty-three

Retirement

And now, I being 65 years old, the Alaska Railroad retired me. The next spring I started to work for Captain Langley and Jack Reagh. They had boats over on the Kuskokwim River, with headquarters at McGrath. So next spring, the steamboat men went to Anchorage, and then over to McGrath in an airplane. These planes were small and could not go very high, we went through Rainy Pass with McKinley on our right—a very beautiful sight.

The steamer, "Nenana," and another, were in a slough across from McGrath. We proceeded to get them ready for the season's work. Captain Langley wanted a set of ways built for the boats and barges, and sent into Bethel for the material. We received our freight from the ocean boat at Bethel, some 300 miles below McGrath.

Captain Langley also owned the ocean boat and it could come up the Kuskokwim to Bethel.

We had no trouble on the river. I had a good pilot, Peter Snow. We made three trips, and learning the river was easy for me. Our chief engineer said that I must have a photographic mind to know the river so quickly.

We built a set of ways and a bunk house, boiler house, and a machine shop, using a cabin already there for a cook house. We finished for the season without any trouble and took a plane over to Anchorage, and then outside.

That winter Helen and I looked around for a place to buy, in Los Angeles. We finally found one—the place where I am now living—a duplex at the corner of First and Detroit Streets. It is a very nice place. That spring we moved in before I left for McGrath.

The spring of 1943 Morrison & Knudson Co. leased the boats from Langley and Reagh, and I found them very fine people to work for—could not be better.

We were very busy that season. The U.S. Army had come to Bethel and they built an airplane field close to our landing where we had built a warehouse. We had to take the material to build another air field part way up the river and one at McGrath also. The Army established posts at these two places and we were very, very busy—hauled the boats and barges out on the ways and then out home.

It was so good to get to a home of our own, and we had a good time that winter, buying furniture and things for it.

Into the Kuskokwim again next spring, and on the way over from Anchorage to McGrath, in the airplane, we got in a thick snow storm at Rainy Pass. The pilot took a chance and dropped down a few feet, and believe it or not, he got under the thick storm, and we made it out of the Pass—a narrow escape that time.

We were very busy transporting Army supplies and soldiers. On one of our trips, we brought up for the Army two barge loads of high grade gasoline, 700 tons—the gasoline in 50-gallon drums. We stopped at a good safe bank, high enough so it would be safe from high water. Under our contract the Army had to unload it. A sergeant came and told me that it was too much work to unload the gas on that bank. He said, "Take it up to that bar and low bank." I asked him, "What if the river should rise and float it off?" I told him we might get rain above, but he would not listen to me. So the soldiers rolled the drum off on that low ground, very easy, and they had a good time.

One dark night halfway up on our last trip, I was on watch, and with the searchlight saw a lot of driftwood, or something, in the river. Thinking something might get into our wheel, we tied up. When daylight came I saw a lot of gasoline drums floating in the river which had risen a lot. Some of the drums were stuck in the sand bars and others went down the slough. We picked up quite a few off of bars and took them to McGrath. Some small boats got a lot, taking them up to the Army.

Morrison & Knudson were now through with the boats—the Army supplies being all delivered. They sent the purser and me out by way of Fairbanks then to Juneau and to Seattle, and on the train home.

The next season we had to take a lot of Army supplies down to Bethel. Afterwards things became very quiet on the river and I did not go back. The plane that brought us to Anchorage was much better than usual and did not go through Rainy Pass—flew away above it.

That winter Helen and I wanted a new car, so we traded in our old one. We went on the train to Buick Co. and bought a new Buick. We drove to Toronto, Ottawa, Montreal, Quebec, down to Key West and on home—a very nice trip.

That spring, Mr. Cunningham, the Superintendent of the Alaska Railroad, wrote and asked me if I could help him out. He needed a pilot very badly. I went back for him for another season and then my steamboat days were over, I was all through working—just stayed home with my dear Helen.

I forgot to say that several years back, Helen's son, Harry, who was working up at Everett, Washington, at the time, got married to a very fine young girl, Miss Ruth Logan. Her father was Methodist Minister which made it all right with me as I was brought up a strict Methodist. It is seldom that you will meet a couple as fine and good as they are.

And now at the age of 70 I was through working and Helen and I spent many happy years together. Then about 1956 Helen became ill and in November of 1958 she passed away. Mere words cannot say how terrible her going was to me. I just cannot get over it, thinking of her day and night. Perhaps we were too happy together. I do not know how I lived through it—I will never know.

And now in April of 1960, I am all alone in the home Helen and I bought, and I will be 85 on Alaska Day the 18th of October. How true it is that life must go on—and on!

Afterword

On August 26, 2001, exactly 100 years after the unhappy eviction of the Barnette family from the riverboat *Lavelle Young* by Charles W. Adams, a celebration observing a century of life for the city of Fairbanks took place in ceremonies on the deck of the 99 percent restored original wheelhouse from the *Lavelle Young* in Pioneer Park in Fairbanks, in conjunction with the state Department of Transportation, the Pioneers of Alaska, and the Fairbanks Historical Preservation Foundation.

When discussing events of a century ago, C.W. Adams makes many (and some possibly confusing) references to river depths, boat drafts, boilers, stopping for firewood, and so on.

It should be noted that the generic term "riverboat" can be applied to just about anything that is underway on a river. However, in the context of this book, a "riverboat" is a steam-powered, wood-burning, sternwheel-driven boat—neither sidewheel nor propeller driven.

Further, descriptions involving riverboat terminology are not necessarily the same as that of conventional vessels. The sternwheelers (and sidewheelers) were, even in their glory days, a strange and hybrid craft that shocked deep-water sailors for a number of reasons. A few examples:

The Klondike riverboats were made of extremely light construction so as to maintain shallow draft even when loaded with cargo and passengers (three feet was thought to be ideal on Alaska rivers).

The "hogging system" (the structural backbone) consisted of exterior wires or rods reaching from the bow to the stern strung over large posts buried way down in the hull.

A large locomotive boiler was generally installed at the forward end of the boat, either on the main deck or in a pit.

At the stern, steam moved through a long pipe from the boilers at the bow to valves aft that could be opened and closed regulating steam to the engines and controlling water from the river fed through a series of filters and condensers for makeup feed water, or conveyed to miscellaneous pumps and valves for the engines or to house services. Two horizontal engines mounted within the deckhouse attached to each of the great Pitman arms that reached to a crank on either side of the paddlewheel, similar to the old-fashioned steam locomotive.

Obviously, to be on board such a boat and watch the Captain, the Pilot, and the engineers handle her when maneuvering around a bend or into a riverside berth (quite often just a tree or driven post to hold against the current) would be a fascinating and edifying experience. Traversing the river against the current would require care to avoid oncoming drift and a careful playing of eddies to make time. The trip downstream, however, could be traumatic, particularly when pushing several obstinate barges around and over the bars. Handling these boats was no place for the indecisive.

Although basic fundamentals of seamanship and boat handling always are the same, it would be wonderful to be able to observe the Pilot guide the boat to a select location, then to watch the engineer handle his backdown lever, his steam valve, his go-ahead lever as signaled from the bridge, whether by bell (jingle) signals by simple wires or from an engine room telegraph. Capt. Howard Adams, however, when discussing the river, remarked with humor of the ongoing feud between chief engineers and Ship Captains that could cause landing problems.

Sternwheelers generally had five rudders, two behind the paddle-wheel for straight ahead work and three just ahead of the paddlewheel for "flanking" (slipping the stern sideways) when backing down.

Whether it be the Yukon, Missouri, or Mississippi, just as Mark

Twain found out, it took years to learn and to memorize the twists, turns, and shoals that changed with the seasons or due to floods, droughts, and—if nothing else—pure cussedness. The old pilots knew their business and had insight. Horace Bixby, Mark Twain's mentor, once said "You send boys up the Mississippi, men to the Missouri." (The Missouri was full of logs and drift.)

Today the Yukon River has few sternwheelers and all are powered with Diesel engines as are the commercial cargo-carrying steel boats that supply the Yukon River villages and outposts. The sternwheeler of today is a tourist boat only. In the era of *A Cheechako Goes to the Yukon*, 250 riverboats powered by steam engines carried cargo, freight, passengers, and animals anyplace from the mouth of the Yukon at St. Michael to the upper reaches of the river and its tributaries. The Yukon is about 2,300 miles long from its headwaters near Juneau, Alaska, to St. Michael (flowing 1,400 miles in U.S. waters) and the boats used great quantities of firewood cut from trees along the river banks, sometimes by the crew but usually by enterprising riverbank woodcutters who sold the fuel to the boats.

The wheelhouse from the *Lavelle Young* at Pioneer Park in Fairbanks gives some idea of the times. The *Lavelle* was not built as a cargo carrier but as a "snag boat" to clear drift from the Columbia River, and, as Captain Howard Adams said, "she was too deep in draft to be truly effective" on the Yukon. But she served her purpose from inception to the end, about 1920.

The boat's wheelhouse has its own story. The wheelhouse was found, mostly in pieces, in the woods near McGrath in 1972 by a Bureau of Land Management employee. What could be recovered was carried in nets by helicopter to Pioneer Park and reconstructed by the Fairbanks Historical Preservation Foundation between 1994 and 2002.

The original intent of the reconstruction, as proposed by several Fairbanks businessmen, was to build a semi-barge hull with deckhouses, smokestack, and miscellaneous hardware to match the size and appearance of the original *Lavelle Young*, all to be mounted safe from winter effects on the riverbank near downtown Fairbanks. As envisioned, the reconstruction and commercial enterprise eventually would become self-sustaining by renting space for shops, food service, and recreational facilities.

Meanwhile, across a basin from the *Lavelle* wheelhouse, the great sternwheeler *Nenana* sits on a concrete drydock built for the purpose in 1983. The *Nenana* is a true and beautiful steam-driven sternwheel riverboat, and is complete with passenger accommodations, crew quarters, and a luxurious salon all reconstructed between 1987–92. Research has shown her to be the second-largest wooden boat in the world today. She has a superb wheelhouse, a rebuilt boiler, and an overhauled engine room revealing the giant engines and Pitman arms intact.

Although typical maintenance is on-going, the boat is always open for tours in the summer. The main deck, or cargo deck, contains a large diorama tracing the Yukon and showing authentic villages on the riverbank in true scale. Miniature trees, people, boats, and animals are to be seen in and around the villages. A painted background mural by Marilyn Jesmain is awe-inspiring. The diorama alone is worth seeing.

Future work planned on board includes adding additional piping in the boat and installing a pipeline from the nearby Chena River to bring fresh water to the boat's boiler as the initial step in running the engines and turning the paddlewheel at a slow RPM for show purposes.

The *Nenana* was designed in 1932 and built in 1934 at the river town of Nenana for the Alaska Railroad.

Capt. C.W. Adams was first the Captain on *Nenana*, probably taking command in 1934 at which time the steamer *Alice* was semi-retired from service. Howard Adams, the Captain's nephew, served on the *Alice* with his uncle and later become Captain of the *Nenana* through the World War II years.

The final self-powered run for *Nenana* was from the town of Nenana to Fairbanks after her purchase by a Fairbanks entrepreneur in 1957. This was to the last trip on any river for the *Nenana*, and it seems fitting that Capt. Howard Adams, called away from his business in Juneau, was her last Captain.

—Jack Kutz, *Bainbridge Island, June 2002*

INDEX

Celebrating Northern History

After graduating in 1950 from Fryeburg Academy in Maine, Jack Williams (left) arrived in Fairbanks, via California, in 1952, two years before the retirement of Alaska's last great sternwheeler, the Nenana. Over the next half century, Williams developed a keen interest in Alaska history, particularly that of the riverboat era.

In 1987, with crucial help from local government, the state of Alaska, and especially the Pioneers of Alaska, Igloo No. 4 and Auxiliary No. 8, Williams founded the Fairbanks Historical Preservation Foundation, a public nonprofit organization dedicated to the mission expressed in its name. He spent the next ten years directing restoration projects for the foundation, serving as its first chairman and then as executive director.

Williams and the foundation raised $2.4 million for the restoration of the Nenana, which had been berthed in Fairbanks since 1957 and was in desperate need of extensive restoration and refitting. The restored riverboat is now in permanent dry-dock in Fairbanks at Pioneer Park, formerly known as Alaskaland.

"It is certain that if a prediction had been made in 1952 that my future would link me to the life of Capt. C.W. Adams (right), his story, and members of his family, I would have rejected it as beyond impossible," Williams recalled. "Nonetheless, that is exactly what happened.